A Championship Team

The Packers and St. Norbert College in the Lombardi Years

by
Cliff Christl

ISBN 978-0-615-39566-1

Library of Congress Control Number: 2010935844

Published and printed in the United States of America

First edition paperback: October 2010

Cover design by Drew Van Fossen
Printing by Independent Printing Inc., De Pere, Wis.

St. Norbert College Press
100 Grant Street
De Pere, WI 54115-2099
www.snc.edu

Dedication

To my dad, Clifford H. Christl, a decorated soldier, who died when I was just 13 days old. He served in the Army for four years during World War II and spent 14 months fighting in Europe. As a staff sergeant in the 11th Armored Division, also known as "The Thunderbolts," he was part of Gen. George Patton's Third Army and fought in the Battle of the Bulge. But before my dad went overseas he attended Chemical Warfare School and later was exposed to radioactive material at Camp Cooke, Calif. He was diagnosed with cancer within seven months after he was honorably discharged from the Army, following the war, and died April 4, 1947, at the Veterans Administration Hospital in Hines, Ill. My dad was born in 1919 at the St. Mary's Mothers and Infants Home in Green Bay and adopted 10 months later by Peter and Martha Christl of Appleton. He attended St. Joseph Grade School and graduated from Appleton High School in 1937.

"All GIs have their own rating system of each other," Parker Schultz, one of his Army buddies, once wrote me. "Our system was very simple. If you had to be in a foxhole during combat who would you choose for a partner? A guy like Cliff would be my first choice."

Acknowledgements

Most of the material in this book was gleaned through interviews with more than 50 people and from my own collection of stories from my years at the Green Bay Press-Gazette, and both The Milwaukee Journal and Journal Sentinel. But a lot of historical data—mostly dates, times, places, transactions, etc.—also was uncovered by looking through microfilm of the Press-Gazette at the Miriam B. and James J. Mulva Library on the St. Norbert College campus. And almost all of the stories on the Packers that appeared in the paper between 1959 and 1968 were written by Art Daley and Lee Remmel, each of whom covered the team for three decades or more. Mike Counter, director of media relations at St. Norbert College, was a big help and so was Mary Jane Herber of the Brown County Library. Other valuable sources were the Buildings and Memorials *booklet published by St. Norbert and the* Green Bay Packers 2009 Media Guide. *But the biggest help of all was my wife, Shirley Christl, who as always was understanding and supportive as I plowed through this project.*

— Cliff Christl

✤

Table of Contents

Table of Contents

❖

Foreword

Here at St. Norbert College, we treasure two iconic photographs. Both, as it happens, feature the college's second president, Fr. Dennis Burke.

The first photograph was taken in 1960. It shows Fr. Burke strolling next to a young John F. Kennedy in front of Boyle Hall. Kennedy was at the time a first-term senator from Massachusetts who was rather audaciously running for the Democratic nomination for president. He was on the St. Norbert campus for an appearance during the Wisconsin primary, and while the candidate is bundled up against the winter cold (there is snow on the ground), Fr. Burke, as usual, is clad simply in his Norbertine white robe.

The second photo is from 1963. It shows Fr. Burke standing next to Green Bay Packers' coach Vince Lombardi outside the entrance to Sensenbrenner Hall as the Packers begin their annual summer camp. Overhead is a banner that reads, "St. Norbert College Welcomes the Champion Packers." This time it's the middle of summer, and Lombardi is wearing a casual, short-sleeved shirt. Fr. Burke again is wearing his full Norbertine white robe—his dress for all seasons.

It's altogether fitting that Fr. Burke figures in these images, for on this campus he too was a larger-than-life presence. Perhaps more than any other individual, it was Fr. Burke who made St. Norbert the modern institution of higher education it is today.

Fr. Burke assumed the presidency in 1955 after having served many years as the right-hand man to our founder, Abbot Bernard Pennings.

By all accounts, Fr. Burke was a true presence. A tall, imposing man who commanded any environment he entered, he had firm opinions on things—including how a Catholic liberal arts college should be operated. Long before business experts talked about "management by walking around," Fr. Burke was apt to turn up anywhere on campus to see first-hand what was going on. But that's also because he was sociable, a man with a ready laugh who could tell a good story and enjoyed one in return.

More important, he was a person of vision. The campus had just become co-educational when he took over, and Fr. Burke said St. Norbert must plan for continuing growth of an enrollment that one day would reach 2,000 students. In the late Fifties that must have struck a lot of people as unrealistic, if not downright nutty. But his prescience meant we were able to accommodate all those new students when in fact they did show up.

Fr. Burke also had the considerable challenge of steering the campus through the Sixties as events at home and abroad rattled every conceivable tradition and convention. John Kennedy went on to become the first (and still lone) Catholic elected President of the United States, only to be assassinated in 1963. The Second Vatican Council was ushering in numerous reforms that reverberate through the Church to this day. The civil rights movement, the women's movement and burgeoning opposition to the war in Vietnam were politicizing campuses all over the nation in unprecedented ways, and St. Norbert wasn't immune. It was a lot for a president to navigate.

And then there were the Packers.

In 1958, Scooter McClean was named to coach the much-loved local heroes who nonetheless had fallen on difficult times. It was Fr. Burke who cut a deal with McClean for St. Norbert to serve as the team's summer home.

Alas for Scooter, he lasted just that one year. His replacement was an alternately gruff and charming New Yorker named Vince

Lombardi. Lombardi was a devout Catholic who had been educated by Jesuits. He immediately liked the Norbertines, and in particular Fr. Burke, a fellow authority figure with whom he struck up a fast and enduring friendship. Relaxed and at home on a college campus, Lombardi would continue and formalize the Packers-St. Norbert relationship.

And more than half a century later, this remains the longest training-camp partnership between a college and an NFL franchise. We at St. Norbert College are tremendously proud of that fact.

When I arrived on campus in 2008, I immediately began to hear the St. Norbert-centric stories about Lombardi and the Packers of that championship era. Indeed, more than four decades after he left, Lombardi remains a visceral presence here; for some of our longer-resident characters, such as Fr. Rowland De Peaux, the memories of the legendary coach are as vivid as if he had been walking the grounds just last week, flashing that hundred-watt grin. Unfortunately, we had no real record of that remarkable decade on our campus, when the Packers were turning Green Bay into Titletown U.S.A. and St. Norbert College was quickly becoming the team's home away from home.

I wanted us to document those stories and memories before we lost any more of them. So we asked veteran sportswriter and author Cliff Christl, who covered the Packers for years, to talk to as many former Lombardi-era players, coaches and staff members as he could find, as well as long-serving Norbertines, faculty members and friends of St. Norbert College who were part of those "glory years." Cliff was indefatigable in reaching these folks, and the stories inside this book are theirs, told in their own words. The focus is confined to the Lombardi years; he stopped coaching the Packers after the 1967 season, and in 1969 he decamped for a short-lived stint as coach of the Washington Redskins.

For all the Sixties social upheaval mentioned earlier, it should be remembered that those times were certainly more innocent, too. One is struck time and again by the sheer sweetness of many of the stories here—the interaction between the Packers and the campus neighbors; local kids running errands for the players; the post-curfew highjinks of Paul Hornung and his incorrigible roomie, Max McGee; players driving their own team buses; players singing after the team dinner for their coach's amusement; players patronizing the downtown bars and malt shops. I absolutely love the idea that a huge, burly lineman could be so cowed by Lombardi that he would hide an ice-cream cone behind his back if the coach was coming the other way.

Of course, in today's security-conscious world, when any off-field indiscretion by a pro athlete is Internet fodder within minutes of its occurrence, the public no longer has anything like that easy access to the Packer players during summer camp. Nonetheless, they are not monks, and the young men still do enjoy their time at St. Norbert College. You often see them walking the grounds in the early evening, relaxing after a hard day's workout.

And one thing *definitely* hasn't changed—they still love the St. Norbert food, and lots of it!

We hope and trust the Packers will be our summer guests for many years to come. As long as they are, Vince Lombardi will be with us, too. And as you'll see from many of the tales in this oral history, so will Fr. Burke, who has never really left his beloved St. Norbert College.

— President Thomas Kunkel
St. Norbert College

❧

Introduction

Here's a little known piece of trivia: The Green Bay Packers weren't the first professional football team to train at St. Norbert College. At least one other NFL team used it as a base before the Packers moved their training camp there in 1958.

In 1955, the Pittsburgh Steelers spent a week at St. Norbert in late August, before and after an exhibition game against the Packers at old City Stadium on Green Bay's near east side. I know that because I have a bittersweet childhood memory of the Steelers' stay.

I was eight years old at the time, living in Allouez, and my stepfather took me out to the campus to tour the dormitory and to get autographs.

I still have the worn, yellowed, slightly torn sheet of paper that the players signed. There are 16 signatures on it. The list includes Jim Finks, a veteran quarterback at the time who is in the Pro Football Hall of Fame for his later work as an NFL general manager; Ernie Stautner, who played defensive tackle for the Steelers for 14 years and another Hall of Famer; and Ted Marchibroda, another Steelers quarterback that year who later spent two different stints as head coach of the Baltimore and Indianapolis Colts.

But the biggest name and most valuable autograph on my sheet was Johnny Unitas, who some football historians still consider the greatest quarterback in the history of the NFL. Except, to be perfectly honest, there's one major flaw with his signature.

Unitas was a rookie that year, a ninth-round draft choice out of the University of Louisville, and the Steelers waived him not long after they left De Pere. And when they did, I erased Unitas' name. The outline of it remained visible, and years later after Unitas had set all kinds of records and had led the Colts to NFL championships in 1958 and '59, and to Super Bowl V following the 1970 season, I retraced it. Only a handwriting expert might be able to tell, but I know it's not authentic.

It's not that I've lost sleep over my childhood imprudence or that I ever would have wanted to sell the autograph for profit. But every once in a great while when I come across my small autograph collection from when I was a kid, I still ask myself: "What in the world were you thinking?"

Anyway, that's also my first memory of being on the St. Norbert campus. As a young teenager in the early 1960s, I returned many times for basketball games at cramped Van Dyke Gym. St. Norbert had some top-notch teams at the time, and for someone like me who was crazy about sports, it was a joy watching them. In both 1961 and '62, St. Norbert qualified for what was then the prestigious National Association of Intercollegiate Athletics tournament in Kansas City, Mo. And in 1963, it had a first-team Associated Press Little All-American in Mike Wisneski, a pint-sized guard and ball-handling wizard.

My next recollection of being on campus dates to 1974. That was my first year covering the Packers for the Green Bay Press-Gazette and it also was the year of a bitter strike by NFL players.

As rookies arrived at St. Norbert on July 9 for the start of camp, a band of veterans was given permission by the Packers to speak to them that evening for an hour at the Minahan Science Building and I was hanging around to cover it all.

Ken Bowman, a holdover from the 1960s and one of the former players interviewed for this book, was the Packers' player representative at the time and led the contingent that addressed the rookies. Two days later, Bowman and two other veterans, Clarence Williams and Keith Wortman, were ordered off the campus by security guards.

A decree handed down by former St. Norbert president Neil Webb banned the players and the public from the campus, or at least the area where the rookies walked to and from dinner, and to and from the buses that took them to practice.

I still have memories of walking the nearby streets in the early evening hours, notebook in hand, as veterans waited to corral any rookies who might stray off campus.

The NFL Players Association finally agreed to a cooling-off period a month later, veterans reported back to work and order was restored at training camp sites across the country.

But just as relationships were changing in football about that time, they were in my business, too. Newspapers had started to adopt strict ethics codes that either discouraged or prevented reporters from accepting even snacks and drinks from the teams they covered. And in the wake of the Watergate scandal, many sportswriters became much more aggressive and critical in their coverage.

No longer were they invited—nor did many young reporters care to attend—social events such as the 5 o'clock gatherings that were held on the St. Norbert campus in the 1960s and which you'll learn more about in this book. In the past, writers also had been free to eat with the Packers at their training table, and that stopped.

So I spent very little time on the St. Norbert campus during the 10 years that I covered the team for the Press-Gazette, during the brief time I was sports editor at the paper or during the many years I wrote about it for The Milwaukee Journal and later the Journal Sentinel.

The one exception was during another NFL players strike in 1982. Over the two months the league shut down that fall, the Packers' veterans who stuck around Green Bay worked out regularly on the St. Norbert campus. And I spent a week working out with them—running sprints on the football practice field; and playing basketball and racquetball, and lifting weights at the Schuldes Sports Center—for a long feature article I wrote for the Press-Gazette.

For whatever reason, I also don't remember ever setting foot on the campus during training camp when Vince Lombardi was coaching. But I grew up with the Lombardi Packers, attended almost all their home games, at least until I went away to college in the fall of 1965, and sat and froze through all three of the NFL championship games they played at Lambeau Field during that period. Yes, I was actually there for the Ice Bowl and still have my $12 ticket stub in Section 18 to prove it.

Plus, I've spent countless hours researching that era and interviewing players from it for other projects that I've undertaken in the past.

That's why I jumped at the offer to write this book when it was extended to me by St. Norbert president Tom Kunkel.

I knew it would be a rewarding undertaking.

CHAPTER 1

Two August Men, One Glorious Era

Fr. Dennis M. Burke was a big man with big dreams.

Standing 6 feet 4 inches, Burke oversaw a period of tremendous growth and enduring change during his 13 years as president of St. Norbert College. Much of it—the addition of 11 new buildings, an enrollment that more than doubled, an endowment fund that soared from $73,000 to $1.7 million and the establishment of a lay Board of Trustees, just to hit the highlights—was spawned by Burke's broad vision and conceptual planning. But, no doubt, even he never imagined what would result from his efforts to lure the Green Bay Packers to the St. Norbert campus during the winter of 1958.

When the executive committee of the Packers voted to move the team's training camp from what is now the University of Wisconsin-Stevens Point to St. Norbert on Feb. 24, 1958, the franchise was in a free fall and the worst of it was yet to come.

Seven weeks earlier, the Packers had fired Coach Lisle Blackbourn and replaced him with Ray "Scooter" McLean. The change came after they had finished 3-9 and in last place in the National Football League's Western Conference. It marked the ninth straight year that the Packers had failed to post a winning record, and the coaching change was the third in eight years. Then the bottom fell out in 1958 as the Packers stumbled and bumbled their way to their worst season ever, sinking to a 1-10-1 record, and McLean was jettisoned after just one season.

Enter Vincent Thomas Lombardi.

Over the next nine years, the Packers won five National Football League championships, including the first two Super Bowls. In turn, Green Bay became a football heaven and Lombardi a sainted coach.

Linked to it all was St. Norbert College.

The Packers launched each of those nine seasons, from 1959 through 1967, by gathering on the school's campus and using it as a temporary base of operations for two months or more. For most of the summer, coaches, players and staff members met there, ate there, slept there and conducted business there. Above all, they bonded there and worked on creating the chemistry that helped the Lombardi Packers become one of the foremost dynasties in pro football history.

The players also found time to have some fun there. Or at least some of their schemes to find fun were hatched there.

"We had some wonderful times there," said Jerry Kramer, a member of all nine of Lombardi's teams.

***

Founded in 1919, the Packers prepared for their first 27 seasons by holding pre-season practices in Green Bay. The only exception was in 1935 when they spent a week at Pinewood Lodge, near Rhinelander, before embarking upon a series of exhibition games across northern Wisconsin.

After the Packers purchased Rockwood Lodge, located just south of Dyckesville, in 1946, they held their first extended training camp beyond the city limits of Green Bay. The lodge had been built by the Norbertine Fathers in 1937 as a community social retreat. With its bucolic setting, shoreline views and stately look, it fulfilled its purpose at first. Then use of it fell off dramatically during World War II and it was put up for sale.

Coincidently, Curly Lambeau, co-founder of the Packers and their authoritative coach, was looking for a year-round training and living quarters for his players at about the same time and was able to convince the team's executive committee to purchase the property for

$32,000. His big plans for Rockwood were soon dashed when it was discovered that the bedrock just beneath the thin layer of topsoil caused shin splints and other injuries. As a result, Lambeau often had to take his team into Green Bay to practice. Nevertheless, the Packers continued to live and train at Rockwood until it was destroyed by fire in January 1950.

The following summer, the Packers practiced on the fields beyond Green Bay East High School, stayed at the old Northland Hotel in downtown Green Bay and ate at the nearby YWCA cafeteria.

Then in 1951, Coach Gene Ronzani decided to take the team out of town again and chose the North Central Experimental Station, located in Grand Rapids, Minn., as its new training site. The Experimental Station was an agricultural school and part of the University of Minnesota system. Considering Grand Rapids was more than 80 miles northwest of Duluth and that a prized herd of Guernseys, as well as hogs and sheep, roamed not far from the practice fields, while swarms of mosquitoes nearly ate the players alive, it was not a popular choice. But, again, the Packers went back for two more summers.

"It was the hell up there and gone," said Art Daley, who covered the Packers for the Green Bay Press-Gazette from the 1940s through the Lombardi era. "I remember driving up there and seeing a little creek that said 'Mississippi River.' You're almost to Canada up there."

When Blackbourn replaced Ronzani as coach, he considered four different sites in Wisconsin before settling on Stevens Point. One of the other places on his list was St. Norbert. But it wasn't available until mid-August because of summer school and other activities that required use of the only dormitory on campus at the time. Stevens Point remained the Packers' summer home for all four years of Blackbourn's reign.

The Packers' move to St. Norbert in 1958 was worked out by Burke and Verne Lewellen, a former star player who was then the general manager of the team.

The agreement called for the Packers to use Sensenbrenner Hall as their living quarters, to eat in Berne Hall—later renamed Burke Hall—and to have access to Boyle Hall for meetings.

19

McLean was elated at the prospect of holding training camp close to home.

"It's wonderful to come home again and it'll be a great morale factor for the entire team," he said when the announcement was made.

While that may have been true, it didn't work out under McLean's lax leadership.

***

L ombardi was hired as McLean's successor on Jan. 28, 1959. He had been backfield coach of the New York Giants from 1954 to 1958, but he hadn't been a head coach since high school. And while Lombardi came highly recommended by NFL commissioner Bert Bell and others, he was somewhat of an unknown and a surprise choice. But he didn't lack for confidence. "I have never been associated with a loser and I don't expect to be now," he vowed.

Lombardi moved quickly to hire assistant coaches and to change the climate around the office, but it took him almost two months to decide on a training camp site. The Giants had trained far away from home at Willamette University in Salem, Ore., for three of the years when Lombardi was on their staff, and at St. Michael's College in Winooski, Vt., for the other two. But despite invitations to hold camp in Stevens Point, Ripon and other places, Lombardi chose to return to St. Norbert, which was less than seven miles from the Packers' stadium and practice field.

"The facilities at St. Norbert College are excellent and close to home," Lombardi said at the time of the announcement.

There was a much different feel to the campus then as compared to now, but there were still plenty of things for Lombardi to like.

St. Norbert was a Catholic liberal arts college that had been founded in 1898 by the Norbertine order to prepare men for the priesthood. In turn, Lombardi was a devout Catholic who made a habit of attending Mass every day.

While the campus may have been short on certain facilities at the time, most notably a student union with a large dining hall, it offered solitude and convenience, two musts on any coach's shopping list. And for Lombardi there were some hidden benefits. There was a chapel in the basement of Sensenbrenner Hall, where the Packers stayed, and the home on Sunset Circle in Allouez that he would move into by the start of the season was less than three miles away.

The St. Norbert campus was much smaller back then—but, there again, small was good if you were a coach who wanted to keep close tabs on your players.

There were only 11 buildings in 1959 and they were all located between Third Street and the banks of the Fox River, and between Grant and Marsh streets. There was Main Hall, St. Joseph Church and the buildings adjacent and kitty-corner, Boyle Hall, Van Dyke Gym, the maintenance building, Berne Hall, a smaller Abbot Pennings Hall of Fine Arts, a nameless science building that resembled a Quonset hut, and Sensenbrenner, which was just three years old.

Five more buildings would be built before Lombardi left Green Bay: Sensenbrenner Memorial Union, Victor McCormick Hall, Mary Minahan McCormick Hall, Bergstrom Hall and the John R. Minahan Science Building.

In Lombardi's time, the Packers used only two of the buildings on a regular basis: Sensenbrenner Hall and the Union, which was completed in 1961.

But they also used the Quonset hut for meetings in the early years, Berne as a cafeteria before the Union opened, and Van Dyke for physical exams until 1966. There are people who were on campus at the time who also remember Lombardi having a room in Victor McCormick sometime after it was completed in 1963; and one or two others mentioned that he may have had one in Main Hall or Berne prior to that.

Then there was the street grid that gave the campus more of an urban than park-like look, and made it more pedestrian-friendly for players looking to walk down to Main Avenue in West De Pere for a haircut or a beer or a frozen treat—or just to hang out.

Second Street ran north and south from Reid Street to Stewart Street; Grant extended beyond Third, east to the river; and Millar

Street ran from Third to Second, if not beyond. Sprinkled about were several older homes that were either located within or adjacent to the campus.

The house many Packers from the Sixties vividly recall was white-framed and located at the northwest corner of Second and Millar. "Old Ed" Longteau, an eccentric, lifelong bachelor lived there. Old Ed would sit in a padded chair in his driveway almost every day of camp, greeting the players and coaches, and engaging them in small talk. They all had to pass by Ed's house when they walked from their dorm to the Union. And they all seemed to enjoy the banter.

Lombardi even invited Old Ed to be his guest one time at the Packers' training table.

The year Lombardi stepped down from coaching, Old Ed turned 92. His sister Elsie was five years younger and lived with him. She, too, kept a watchful eye on the Packers.

"Always says, 'Good morning,'" Elsie said of Lombardi in an interview with the Press-Gazette in 1968. "But he keeps his distance with his players. And I'll tell you, those boys toe the line and stay out of trouble."

Although the Packers moved out before fall classes began, there also were fewer students on campus back then and more Norbertines. The enrollment in 1959 was 976—there were more than 300 Reserve Officers' Training Corps students on campus—compared to 2,175 in the winter of 2010. And priests composed more than 40 percent of the faculty.

But different as it was, the campus was beautifully landscaped and meticulously cared for just as it is today.

"It was always tidy," said Bill Bohne, who has been teaching at the school since 1965. "Burke had this thing about walking on the lawn. It was, 'Don't make paths on the lawn.'"

***

Fr. Burke may have been as revered on the St. Norbert campus as Lombardi was in football circles. Burke lived to the age of 93 and for almost 80 of those years he was connected in some way with St. Norbert. It was his greatest love, although the Packers might have come in a close second.

Just as Burke had negotiated with Lewellen to bring the Packers to St. Norbert in 1958, he dealt with Lombardi to bring them back a year later. And an outgrowth of those talks between Burke and Lombardi was a lasting spiritual and social kinship.

A native of Casco, Wis., a small town in Kewaunee County, Burke moved to De Pere in 1919—the year the Packers were born—to enroll in the old St. Norbert High School. He graduated from there in 1923, graduated from St. Norbert College in 1926 and was ordained as a Norbertine priest in 1929. He joined the college's faculty as a member of the philosophy department in 1932 and became the college's second president in 1955 following the death of Abbot Bernard Pennings.

Burke was a storyteller and a charmer. And his calm personality seemed to mesh perfectly with Lombardi's volatile one.

"He and Burke became hard and fast friends right from the get-go," said Bohne. "There was something that happened there. Fr. Burke, No. 1, was a very engaging Irishman. He was enticing and knew how to engage people. He was good at stroking them, too, making them feel good. I just think they hit it off."

It didn't hurt that Burke was an avid Packers' fan and shared in the joy of Lombardi's victories. And Lombardi was never so respectful and subservient as he was around priests and nuns.

"They had nothing to argue about. They were both Packer fans," joked Fr. Nicholas Nirschl, a mathematics teacher at St. Norbert in the 1960s.

***

Lombardi's first training camp opened in July 1959 with a meeting of nearly 40 rookies, four veteran quarterbacks and more than a dozen other early-arriving veterans. The rest of the veterans reported two days later, increasing the number of players on hand to more than 70.

By all accounts, it was a brutal camp. Practices were filmed for the first time in franchise history and players were closely critiqued during evening meetings at St. Norbert. Early on, veteran defensive tackle Dave Hanner was hospitalized more than once for heat stroke or some similar complication. Players who jumped the gun on their wind sprints were forced to run extra laps one day, players who dropped passes another day.

There were "nutcracker" drills—essentially a test of manhood where a defensive lineman was required to fend off a blocker and attempt to tackle a running back in a confined area. And that wasn't the worst of it. There were killer grass drills where players had to run in place, plop to the ground and jump back up—over and over and over—at Lombardi's barking commands.

Four days into that first camp, all of Lombardi's yelling left him hoarse and he didn't get his voice back for several days. Also within the first week, he swapped popular veteran fullback Howie Ferguson for a draft pick, although the deal was nullified for medical reasons and Ferguson was ultimately forced to retire. By the end of camp, Lombardi also had disposed of three more well-established veterans: halfback Al Carmichael, defensive tackle Jerry Helluin and quarterback Babe Parilli.

Parilli was the victim in the biggest and most important battle of camp. Lombardi started four different quarterbacks in the six exhibition games, including Parilli, and finally settled on Lamar McHan, a six-year veteran who had been acquired in a conditional trade with the Chicago Cardinals. Although moody and paranoid, McHan won the job over Bart Starr, who was deemed by Lombardi, at that point, to be too self-effacing to be an effective leader.

"At that time, the opinion around here and, in fact, the opinion in the league was that Starr would never make it," Lombardi would say five years later. "They said he couldn't throw well enough and he wasn't tough enough and that he had no confidence in himself and that no one actually had any confidence in him."

Starr would replace McHan as the starter late in Lombardi's first season and lead the Packers to victory in four of their last five games, but it wouldn't be until the sixth game of the 1960 season that he permanently won the job.

In all, Lombardi turned over one-third of the roster that first year; 12 of the 36 players who survived the final cut were new.

After departing St. Norbert and spending two more weeks at Oakton Manor on Pewaukee Lake, west of Milwaukee, the Packers entered the season buoyed by their 4-2 record in exhibition games and brimming with confidence that no other team in the league would be better conditioned.

And they had a right to be.

They upset the Chicago Bears, 9-6, in their opener at what was then City Stadium and is now Lambeau Field. They went on to finish 7-5, their best record in 14 years. And Lombardi won NFL Coach of the Year honors in a landslide in voting by the Associated Press.

It was a harbinger of things to come.

***

As training camp neared in Lombardi's second season, it was obvious that forces of change were at work. More than a week before they were scheduled to report, veterans started arriving in Green Bay, champing at the bit to check into the dorms and to start practicing on their own.

"This is very unusual," Jack Vainisi, the team's business manager and chief scout, said at the time. Vainisi was in position to know. He had joined the Packers in 1950 and had lived through the hard times.

But when practice started for the full squad on July 25, Lombardi was no more forgiving than he had been the year before. On the first day of double workouts, the players dropped a total of 670 pounds or about 10 per man. And, once again, Hanner wound up in the hospital.

Lombardi was no less tolerant of players who broke the rules, either. Free agent halfback Dick Posewitz of Sheboygan was proof of that.

Posewitz shone in the annual intra-squad game in early August, rushing for 60 yards in seven carries and scoring a touchdown. Hence, rather than go back to the dorm to meet curfew, he chose to celebrate. Posewitz had a teammate stuff pillows under his sheet in his dorm room, while he took off for Sheboygan to drink beer with his buddies at Bratwurst Day.

Posewitz's celebration ended within 24 hours when Lombardi placed him on waivers.

***

Sort through all the lore, all the amusing tales of Lombardi's training camps, and there's perhaps no better story than the one that unfolded in the first 24 hours after rookies reported in 1961.

They came in on a Sunday evening, took physicals—for most of Lombardi's reign those were conducted on the campus—and an 18th-round draft pick, chosen as a future the year before, named Royce Whittington topped the scales at 319 pounds. That was 54 more than his weight at Southwestern Louisiana.

Whittington, a 6-foot-2 defensive lineman with a greased-back James Dean haircut, was wearing street clothes when he was weighed in by trainer Domenic Gentile. Whittington's short-sleeved, collared shirt was unbuttoned leaving his imposing gut hanging out and over the beltline of his slacks.

Lee Remmel, then a sportswriter for the Press-Gazette, asked Whittington that night why he had put on so much weight. Whittington said that he felt he needed to beef up to play pro football. The next day, the paper planned to run a picture of Whittington and his ample stomach on the front page of its sport section.

But the presses hadn't even started to roll before Whittington was cut. And Remmel raced from the practice field to the office to pull the picture.

Whittington was on his third lap around the Oneida Street field before the start of the 10 a.m. practice when Lombardi spotted him.

"Out! You're out of here!" Lombardi bellowed across the field in Whittington's direction, according to Remmel. "You mean me?"

Whittington signaled. "Yeah, you! You're out!" Lombardi roared again. Clearly, it had to be the shortest career in Packers' history.

***

One of the rituals during Lombardi's training camps was that rookies—and not just rookie players—had to sing at the evening meal. In 1962, one of the most popular singers was 10-year-old Pat Fears, son of ends coach Tom Fears and a training room helper. Pat drew loud cheers for his rendition of *Old McDonald Had A Farm*.

With the Packers coming off their first NFL title under Lombardi and preparing for the annual College All-Star Game, more media heavyweights than ever started showing up in Green Bay. And in all likelihood, nearly all of them attended the 5 o'clock cocktail hour on the St. Norbert campus or dined there or both. Some also may have slept in the dorm.

Red Smith, a Green Bay native who would later win a Pulitzer Prize for his sports columns, covered more than one of Lombardi's camps. Another prominent visitor was Tex Maule of Sports Illustrated.

It was in 1962 that W.C. Heinz, one of the great craftsmen of all-time, spent several weeks in Green Bay gathering material for *Run to Daylight,* the book that he and Lombardi were collaborating on. Dick Schaap, then working for Newsweek, also came on assignment.

That also was the summer that rookie tackle John Sutro allowed his ego to balloon after matching up against future Hall of Fame defensive end Willie Davis in an early pass rush drill. Davis didn't go all out and Sutro managed to hold his own against him. Sutro's mistake was boasting about it.

"I'm surprised Davis wasn't as tough as I thought he'd be," he told veteran tackle Forrest Gregg after practice. About as fast as someone could snap a towel in the locker room, Davis was being razzed by his fellow veterans about some rookie who had handled him in practice. This went on for a day or so—in the locker room, the dorm or wherever—and it had Davis itching for a rematch.

"I was pretty hot by the time we lined up again," he said. And as

Davis remembered it, this time it really was a mismatch. Naively, Sutro went back to Gregg afterward and told him, "Something made Davis mad." It probably was a blessing in disguise that shortly thereafter Sutro was shipped to Dallas for a draft pick.

On a completely different front, in early August, the first Vince Lombardi Scholarship to St. Norbert was awarded to Gordon Sauer, a basketball and baseball player at Milwaukee Custer High School.

***

In the 1960s, training camp lasted two months or more, with the first two weeks devoted to two-a-days and the rest of it scheduled around five or six exhibition games. There were no minicamps or off-season conditioning programs.

Players generally didn't come to camp in shape; they came to get in shape, as Max McGee attested upon his arrival in 1963.

"This afternoon was the first time I've run since I trotted off the field at Yankee Stadium last winter," McGee said in reference to the 1962 NFL championship game.

While training camp technically lasted nine weeks in 1963, the Packers spent a week of it in Dallas. Following an exhibition game in Miami against the Pittsburgh Steelers, the Packers flew to Dallas and practiced there before playing the Cowboys in another exhibition.

That wasn't unusual at the time. Exhibition games were often played in small, non-NFL cities and teams tried to limit their traveling. So there were some lengthy stretches in those early years where the Packers were technically in camp, but somewhere other than St. Norbert.

In 1962, they left for almost 10 days when they had back-to-back exhibitions in Dallas and Jacksonville, Fla. In 1963, the Packers played a game in New Orleans and then flew to Bear Mountain, N.Y., for a week of training before playing the Giants in Jersey City.

And in 1959, they flew to San Francisco for a game and then spent a week in Portland, Ore., before playing another game there. Later they flew to Bangor, Maine, for a game and then headed to

Greensboro, S.C., for almost a week before playing in Winston-Salem, N.C.

But starting in 1964, that all changed. The Packers started playing more exhibitions in Green Bay and Milwaukee, and playing their away games almost exclusively in other NFL cities. After that, their road trips usually lasted only one or two nights.

Along with the national writers who started showing up more often in Green Bay as Lombardi achieved more success, so did college football coaches.

One of the visitors in 1963 was a little known assistant coach at Florida State named Bobby Bowden. The next year both Woody Hayes, the legendary Ohio State coach, and Bo Schembechler, then coaching at Miami of Ohio and not yet the legend he became at Michigan, came, but on different days. In fact, Hayes attended a civic luncheon held for the Packers on the St. Norbert campus. The luncheon was first held in 1963 and it continued throughout Lombardi's stay with the Packers.

The rookie who might have made the biggest hit singing in the dining hall that year was 41-year-old Pat Peppler, the team's new director of player personnel. Peppler attended high school in Shorewood, a suburb of Milwaukee, and was well acquainted with Wisconsin winters. So he composed his own song, "Ode to an Eskimo."

***

The made-for-television documentary *Run to Daylight,* an offshoot of the book done by Heinz and Lombardi, was filmed in the early days of training camp in 1964 and many of the scenes were shot on the St. Norbert campus.

The film started with Lombardi walking along the campus mall and greeting two nuns. There was another scene of Lombardi and Peppler welcoming the rookies to camp at the steps of Sensenbrenner Hall. And perhaps the most captivating scene was that of Lombardi delivering his opening address to the team at St. Norbert.

Lombardi stood at a lectern and, as always, spoke in a clear, crisp voice and with his emotions seemingly pouring from every word.

Here was his message:

"First, I'd like to welcome you all, of course, and tell you how proud we are to have you as part of the Packers, just as you should be proud to be here and be part of this team. One thing about the Packers is that it's a team with a great tradition; a great and wonderful tradition. And that tradition, or whatever you want to call it, that glory that is the Packers has been developed through one thing only and that's pride. Everybody has ability, but pride and performance is what makes the difference. Now, how do you develop pride? Pride is developed by a winning tradition. That's how it's developed: By a winning tradition. Actually, the only difference between anyone in this league, any one person in this league, any player in the league, any team in the league, is in energy. This is a tough and it's a cruel business. We have to produce. I'm only here, Red's only here, we're only here because we win. Period. And when we lose, we're gone. Therefore, we have to win. Therefore, you have to win. And we only want winners. Now, one other thing please. Fatigue makes cowards of us all. You can't play fatigued. Therefore, it's up to you to be in prime physical condition. I can't put you in physical condition. I can start you. You've got to keep yourself in prime physical condition because a fatigued player is a coward. He can't go 100 percent."

Howard Cosell was on campus during the shooting and conducted the interviews. David Maraniss in his best-selling book, *When Pride Still Mattered: A Life of Vince Lombardi*, said Heinz, who was back for several more weeks that summer, told him that Lombardi had said Cosell was "a pain in the neck." But Lou Volpicelli, the director of the documentary, said he didn't notice any obvious signs of friction between the two. And Cosell in his book, *Cosell*, admitted to just one confrontation with Lombardi on the practice field.

Cosell also wrote that Lombardi opened up to him about two other subjects during his stay in Green Bay.

One was his requirement that rookies had to sing at dinner, a form of hazing.

"It's good for them," Lombardi told Cosell. "Embarrasses them a little, but relieves them a lot. Makes them part of a group."

Cosell said he also sat on a bank of the Fox River and listened to

Lombardi talk about how difficult it was to cut a player.

Cosell quoted Lombardi as saying: "When a kid has given you the best he has to give, and you have to tell him it wasn't good enough, that's when you ache inside and think maybe there's a better way to make a living, maybe football isn't worth it." Lombardi added that the worst part was telling a longtime veteran he was through. "You can't face him, you don't know how to tell him, but you have to," Lombardi said. "I've had to do that, and I don't mind telling you, I've cried."

***

It wasn't often that Lombardi had to put his players on strict diets. Few of them ever showed up at his camps grossly overweight. But defensive tackle Leon Crenshaw was an exception in 1967. Crenshaw, a 6-4 defensive lineman from Tuskegee University who had gained experience with a semipro team in Lowell, Mass., reported at 315 pounds. Thanks to a diet and Lombardi's demanding drills, Crenshaw dropped 37 pounds in five weeks and made it to the final cut before he was waived.

Crenshaw also was one of several rookies who raised the level of entertainment that summer. Crenshaw and first-year backfield coach Tom McCormick could both carry a tune. Ten-year-old P.J. O'Hara, an equipment aide and the son of one of Lombardi's close friends in New York, brought the house down one night with a rendition of *Be Kind to Your Web-Footed Friends*. And rookie fullback Jim Mankins wowed everyone with his harmonica solo, *You Are My Sunshine*.

Crenshaw, by the way, returned the next year and made the team, but lasted only one season in the NFL.

Five days before camp ended in 1967, Lombardi spoke at the sixth annual Packer recognition luncheon in the Union and expressed optimism that the Packers would make history that season.

"This year, we face the greatest challenge we've ever faced," Lombardi told his audience. "We will be in quest of an unprecedented third straight championship, something no team has ever done. I believe we have the wherewithal to do it."

The Packers won their third NFL title on the afternoon of New Year's Eve, beating the Dallas Cowboys, 21-17, on Bart Starr's frozen-in-time quarterback sneak in the Ice Bowl, a game for the ages and one that has come to define the franchise. The Packers followed that up two weeks later by winning Super Bowl II over the Oakland Raiders.

Thus, they became the first team ever to win three straight titles since the NFL went to a playoff format in 1933. The only other time a team won three straight was when the Packers ruled the league from 1929 to 1931, when championships were decided by the final standings.

With this crowning achievement in hand, Lombardi stepped down as the Packers' coach on Feb. 1, 1968. He remained general manager through the following season and then left for Washington to become coach of the Redskins. Fr. Burke's career followed a similar course that year. He retired as St. Norbert president and assumed the more honorary position of chancellor.

Lombardi died of cancer in 1970 at age 57. Burke died in 1998 at age 93.

But their legacies have yet to die.

CHAPTER 2

The Norbertines

FR. BRENDAN McKEOUGH

McKeough taught economics at St. Norbert College from 1953 to 1978 except for a brief period while he attended graduate school at Marquette University. A native of Fond du Lac, McKeough graduated from St. Norbert in 1947 and was ordained in 1953. He is semi-retired and living at St. Joseph Priory. A life-long Packers fan, he remembers attending a game as early as 1936 and retains vivid memories of a game against the Chicago Bears played in 1939 at City Stadium, located behind East High School.

I remember it was Sid Luckman's first game. The Packers won, 21-16. At that time, the other team dressed at the Northland Hotel, then walked right in and we'd walk right in with them at the south gate. On the way out, I remember standing there to watch the Bears file out and Luckman was in tears. He was a rookie. Apparently, some of the older Bears yelled at him. I remember he said, "It wasn't all my fault." [So] I grew up with Packer blood.

(Luckman played quarterback for the Bears from 1939 to 1950. He was inducted into the Pro Football Hall of Fame in 1965. The nine-story Hotel Northland was located at 304 N. Adams St. in downtown Green Bay. The building is still standing.)

It was Fr. Dennis Burke who brought the Packers to St. Norbert. He was a big Packer fan. He had a seat for a long, long time, the last row under the press box. He and Lombardi were close pals. He and Lombardi would drive together when Lombardi was giving a talk in Milwaukee. He'd say, "Me and Vince, we're going to Milwaukee tomorrow." For a while [Burke] had a house over on Third Street, but he lived here [in the priory] most of the time. He had so much contact with Lombardi, more than anybody. Vince was very Catholic. He liked priests. And Dennis was so easy to get along with. He was very affable. Lombardi was too, I think, when he wasn't coaching. I'm sure Fr. Burke was the prime mover. He would have bent over backwards to get the Packers here. And he was in a position to do it. He was the boss around here. He was arguably a greater Packer backer than I was.

We'd see Lombardi all the time [during training camp]. We were here and [the Packers] were there *(he said as he sat in St. Joseph Priory and pointed south.)* Sometimes we even ate near them. I remember a time when they were redoing our kitchen, so we had to eat over there [in the Union]. That time, we saw them every night for a couple months.

They lived in Sensenbrenner Hall and down in the basement was a chapel. Of course, Vince—I understand since when he went to grade school—always went to Mass at 7 o'clock in the morning: through high school, through college, when he was at West Point, when he was with the [New York] Giants. At that time, we had a priest on every floor. That was their residence year round. Fr. Ernie La Mal was on that floor near that chapel. He would have 7 o'clock Mass and Vince was the server. Vince always served Mass. Well, Fr. La Mal was going to be gone on vacation for a couple of weeks, so he asked me if I'd take the Mass. Sure. If Vince Lombardi is going to be my server, I can take over his Mass. That was where I met [Lombardi]. He was more than on time. He was there before I got there. He organized everything for the Mass. You know, each priest has their little idiosyncrasies. We all do things a little differently. And after the first day, he knew exactly how I liked it. He had it all down pat. Then we'd have a chance to chat before Mass was done. There weren't many guys who came. Phil Bengtson was there every morning. And the only two players I remember being there all the time were Zeke Bratkowski and Bob Skoronski. But, by the way, Vince was always very attentive serving Mass. He was like a little boy serving Mass.

As far as I know, during training camp, Vince always went to Mass here. I'm pretty sure he lived at home, but I remember one morning we were waiting for Mass and he was standing at a window on ground level looking out and he said, "It's my wedding anniversary and here I am." But wedding anniversary or not, he wasn't going to break his routine. Although he did one time; he broke his rule. Dudley Birder, our great music man here, put on *My Fair Lady* during the summer and it was so well done. Even a Chicago critic came up and said it was better than anything he had seen on Broadway. Vince broke his rule and went to see *My Fair Lady*.

The big event that happened during that time was the [New York] Giants were coming to town for an exhibition game on a Saturday night and Vince came to me and said, "We'll have Mass on Saturday morning and the owner, Wellington Mara, is coming with his wife." [Mara's] brother had died shortly before that. So come 7 o'clock Saturday morning, Vince and Marie, and the two Maras were there for Mass. Suddenly, there is a huge electric storm. We're just ready for Mass and all the lights go out. So we lit extra candles and we're all reading like this (*McKeough said as he squeezed his shoulders, stuck his face forward and squinted.*) Here I was in a huddle with Wellington and Mrs. Mara, and Marie and Vince. Gosh, if I could have a picture. That's my precious memory of Vince.

After the war, the college was looking for equipment and we got an old Quonset hut. They put it up in the yard, just back there behind the priory, along the river. We used it for a lot of classes. And Vince used it at night for his talks. It would be so warm, the door was always open, and we'd sneak out and sit out there and hear him lecturing. It was the biggest room we had at that time. It was ideal. There was a lot of room. It could hold way over 100. I held a lot of classes there. When you had a big class, you'd use it. Or a lot of teachers used it for final exams when they put a couple classes together.

I still remember when [Lombardi would] be lecturing them on

blocking. "You don't just hit that man, you seal him." That was a word he used a lot, "Seal him." He'd say, "You don't just touch him. You seal him." I understand at times, he could use strong language, but I never heard it. But, boy, he was forceful. There was never any doubt about where the message was. We weren't right next to him—maybe 30 feet away—and we caught every word.

We'd be sitting in the grass. Not more than a half-dozen or so of us would go over there. We had a lot of guys from the East and the Packers didn't mean that much to them. But for us Packer backers, it was something. At that time, we wore our white habits all the time unless we were taking a shower or in bed. And we'd just sit on the ground. I don't know if Vince knew we were out there or not. But I don't think he would have cared. He liked priests. I did it as often as I could.

If we'd take a walk, which was kind of customary after we'd eat our meals, we'd bump into Vince maybe. Or we'd see the Packers coming back from lunch. When our kitchen was being repaired and we ate over there, we ate in a room adjacent to where the Packers ate.

I remember somebody was visiting us from the East and he had a little boy who was 8, 9, 10 years old. The Packers had to pass the room where we were eating. Anyway, Bart Starr came in and he evidently knew this man or the man knew him, and the man introduced his little boy to Bart Starr. The little kid was kind of shy, a little nervous, and he said, "You know, I'm an Eagles' fan." Bart was just wonderful. He said, "You are? What a fine team they have." The way he handled that boy was just perfect. But there were other Packers who would sneak out another door and go around—Ron Kramer was one of them—so they could avoid the kids who were waiting to get their autographs. The kids found out the Packers would come out the front door after they ate and they'd wait for them. But we didn't see the players very much. The only time we'd see them is if they were coming out of their evening meal. But we'd see the people waiting, especially the kids. There were always people looking for autographs.

I remember I saw [Paul] Hornung once. I was over in Sensenbrenner and he came down the stairs and we had this memorable conversation.

He said, "Do you know where we put our laundry to have it picked up?" I said, "No, I don't know." That was it. That was my only encounter with Paul Hornung.

But there was one anecdote we heard. The first year Lombardi was here and they were going to get on the bus after breakfast to go to the stadium, Hornung said to Vince, "I have my car. I'll meet you there." Vince said, "If you get in the car, keep going and head south. We all get on the bus." I didn't observe that, but that was one of the stories that circulated. That would be the first year, the first time the bus left with Hornung.

FR. ROWLAND DE PEAUX

De Peaux taught French and Spanish classes at St. Norbert from 1960 to 1991 except for occasional intervals, and also served as prefect and counselor at Sensenbrenner Hall while the Packers were staying there during training camp in the Lombardi era. A native of Green Bay and a 1948 graduate of St. Norbert, De Peaux was ordained in 1951. He remains a professor emeritus at the college and lives at St. Joseph Priory.

I met Mr. Lombardi when he first came to Green Bay. I was teaching at Premontre High School from 1957 to 1960. I think it was only a couple of weeks after he arrived, he gave a talk at Premontre to the Fathers and Mothers Club. I asked Marie, "Do you think you're going to like it in Green Bay?" She said, "Fr. De Peaux, it all depends on one little word: Win, win, win." It was out in the hallway, just Marie and myself. I didn't know Vince real well at that time, but I got to know Marie quite well. She was in the Mothers Club since Vince Jr. was a student and I was the moderator for the Mothers Club. [We] remained very good friends through the years.

I came back here to St. Norbert College in 1960 and taught full time in the foreign language department. I lived in Burke Hall at the time—it was Berne then—but eventually moved to Sensenbrenner, where the Packers lived. That was my residence. But in 1961, '62 before I moved into Sensenbrenner, I had my foreign language lab in the basement.

That was where I had some encounters with Vince Lombardi even before I moved into Sensenbrenner. There was a console room there for playing tapes and the Packers used a huge room next to my language lab for their team meetings.

There was one time when I went into listen to some tapes. Vince heard some noise and thought it was a spy. He came in—I was just in a T-shirt and slacks—and he said *(De Peaux raised his voice at that point)*, "What the heck are..." *(De Peaux then lowered it)*, "Oh, Father, I'm sorry." [Lombardi] was ready to grab me by the chest. I was quite startled. I had my back to him when he came in. He did say, "I thought someone was spying." I looked right into his face and could tell he wasn't happy about somebody being outside the door of his meeting room. I think that was the summer of '61 or '62. One of our other foreign language teachers, a layman, [Lombardi] did grab by the shirt and wondered who he was. He was worried about spies, like they all were.

I used to see Vince in the dorms at times and we'd greet each other. Some people think that he lived in Sensenbrenner during training camp. He lived at home. He went to Mass at St. Willebrord. But sometimes— I don't know how often it was anymore—he'd come early in the morning and we'd have a 7 o'clock Mass in the chapel in the basement at Sensenbrenner. Fr. Burke said the Mass quite often. Sometimes, he'd ask me to say it. And when Lombardi was there, he served the Mass. When I had Mass, it was Lombardi, Phil Bengtson and Zeke Bratkowski. That was usually it.

Those were times I'd see Vince and talk to him. But when he was there, it was very evident that he was all business, outside of the Mass time. So I didn't disturb him. I'd say, "Good morning, Vince," or something like that. But I didn't attempt any chit-chat. I didn't ask, "How's Marie today?" I just didn't feel that was appropriate. He was at work. He was always very cordial, polite. But you could tell, he wasn't one for small talk.

I noticed when Vince was around Sensenbrenner that the players had respect for him and probably fear. But I never saw him lose his temper.

Vince's office was in the basement of Sensenbrenner: the southwest corner. He didn't seem to spend a lot of time there. It was a small office. The coaches had another room where they could meet. It seems to me he'd stop there in the morning. I don't recall him being there in the evening. I'm sure he was staying at home. In fact, one time I asked Marie, "What is it like living with Vince once training camp starts and during the season?" She said, "Father, we don't talk." I said, "Marie, are you serious?" She said, "Yes. We don't talk. He is so intense during the season." She didn't mean that they didn't say good morning. But they didn't have a lot of casual conversation once football started.

The players lived on the first floor and second floor. I lived on second floor. The rookies were on second floor, but I remember Bart Starr being on second floor with Henry Jordan. They roomed together. I'm not sure they used the third floor. It was two in a room.

I'd go into Bart Starr's room. He and Henry Jordan would be sitting there in their shorts before they went to bed at night. I'd see other players and say hello. They knew who I was. I didn't have many long conversations. I'd talk to Bart once in awhile. Later, when Vince was gone, I'd have a lot of conversations with some of the rookies. I became friendly with Scott Hunter. So quite a few would come into my sitting room and talk.

My cousin's three little boys lived in De Pere and were big fans of Bart Starr. I went to see him once and apologized for disturbing him. It was about 8 o'clock or whatever. He and Henry Jordan were sitting there and I told him what I wanted: an autographed picture for these three little boys who admired him so. He said, "Fr. De Peaux, don't apologize. They are our fans. Without them, we are nothing." He was so gracious. He gave me three glossy 8 by 12 autographed pictures. Then one time they came and met him. He had said, "Bring them around some time."

I think some of the assistant coaches stayed there during the Lombardi years. I think the ones who did the bed checks stayed there. I knew they had curfew and one time I was a little embarrassed. I knew Phil Bengtson, too, from Premontre, and Phil poked his head in one time and said, "Father, time for them to be in bed." Phil had kind of a quiet presence, but he exuded some authority.

I never knew about anybody sneaking out, even during the Lombardi era with Paul Hornung and Max McGee. They talk about those two sneaking out, but I was in my room in bed. I'm sure they didn't make a lot of noise. And they were on first floor. I was on second floor.

The players ate in what's called our Union, where the cafeteria is. They ate in the big lounge on the second floor. They had their own dining room, their own waiters or waitresses. But I never went over there to eat. After exhibition games, they would have a gathering or a party upstairs in the Union and sometimes I was invited to that. There would be players there and their wives, all the coaches, some of the media. I remember Bud Lea being there at times. It was very relaxed, especially if they won. They had a lot of food. Vince would be there. I was surprised in that I thought he would be the center of attention, but he would often be off to the side. It seemed that he felt a little uncomfortable being in the presence of his players in that kind of setting. And it seemed to me he didn't stay around too long. The players would be talking and laughing and eating. The team was always winning and the mood was very light. And it seemed that Vince let them do their thing. He wasn't right on top of them.

The 5 o'clock club was held in a room in the basement of Sensenbrenner next to the chapel on the southwest side. If you went out the back door of the chapel and right across from there was a big lounge. That's where they had the 5 o'clock club every day. I was never invited to that. They had drinks and snacks. It was their cocktail hour.

There was a lot of smoking back then. And Vince was almost a chain smoker. Phil smoked, too. I think they smoked when they were watching their films and at their cocktail hour. But I don't recall them walking around the corridors with cigarettes. I never saw Vince with a cigarette when he was walking around or with the players. I don't recall seeing many of the players smoke.

I never heard anybody complain about Lombardi or Bengtson or the coaches. I respected the players for that. They didn't come and sit in my room and bitch. They talked about what they were all about and how things were going, but that it was tough and, for the rookies, how intense it was trying to make the team.

After breakfast in the morning, the players would go to practice. They'd come back and go to lunch. Some of them would rest: put their feet up or lay on their bunk. Then they'd go back for the afternoon practice. Stop at Buck's Bar on the way back. Then they'd have a meeting again. So their leisure time was just to sit and relax, and recoup a little bit.

(Janssen's Tavern, better known as Buck's, was located at 401 Reid Street. The Packers frequented it during the Lombardi years, but it became more popular with the players in the late Sixties and early Seventies.)

The meetings at night would be held in Sensenbrenner. The large room there could maybe seat 100. It was used as a lecture hall for classes. It was a dorm, but there were some classrooms in the basement.

It was kind of a Spartan existence, but it was a relaxed atmosphere. The dorm rooms had a bed on each side. As you entered there was a wardrobe and drawers on each side. There were desks back by the windows. They were your standard dorm rooms.

Sensenbrenner opened in the fall of 1956. So it was the newest dorm on campus. Even when Victor McCormick opened in 1963, they stayed in Sensenbrenner. They were still in Sensenbrenner in 1974. I moved out in '74 because they turned it into a girls' dorm instead of a men's dorm. Eventually, they had their meetings in the John R. Minahan Science Building. I think that was after they left Sensenbrenner, but maybe even during the last couple years they were in Sensenbrenner.

Marie Lombardi wouldn't come on campus very often during training camp. I remember one time she was on campus for a prom or a big dance. I think she and Vince were honorary chairpersons, and they met with the king and queen. But I don't remember her being here very often.

She was a feisty lady, very friendly, but not overly or gushy. Nice lady. Very warm. She knew her mind and what she wanted. She didn't push herself around. She could have been, "I'm Vince Lombardi's wife." But she didn't. She was Marie.

There were times when Vince was in a pensive, contemplative mood when I saw him. I think if he had any dealings with anybody he'd call them to his office.

I wasn't terrified of him. I remember the first time I went in to say 7 o'clock Mass and he was standing there very quietly, I thought, "Oops, my Lord, this is Vince Lombardi." I was a little shaky, a little apprehensive knowing what he was like. But he was very gentle. He'd say, "Father, is it time to light the candles now?" He was like a little altar boy. It seems he could fit into the role that was required. When he was dealing with his team as coach, he was no longer the little altar boy, that's for sure.

He wanted his faith to be private. I remember one time somebody wanted to write an article about his faith and going to daily Mass. He said, "That's my private life." He said his faith was very important to him, that Mass was a big part of his life, but he didn't share much beyond that.

I never saw women hanging around outside Sensenbrenner. I think the coaches watched that pretty carefully.

I didn't see [Vince Jr.] around much. I know for a fact Vince Sr. didn't have much time for his kids once training camp started.

I remember Marie telling me when he gave up the coaching job and stayed as general manager, "He made a terrible mistake." She said, "He never should have given up coaching. That's where he belongs." I think it was shortly after camp started that she told me, "He missed it and knew it was the wrong decision, but he couldn't go back on it because of Phil."

FR. NICHOLAS NIRSCHL

Nirschl taught mathematics at St. Norbert from 1963 to 1972. A native of South Milwaukee, he also graduated from St. Norbert in 1951 and was ordained in 1956. He is retired and living at Santa Maria de la Vid Priory in Albuquerque, New Mexico.

Lombardi attended daily Mass and we had a chapel in Sensenbrenner Hall. Normally, it would be someone else. But I was one of the counselors there, so when the person who had the Mass wasn't there, I would [conduct it] and I would be able to chat with [Lombardi] a little bit. That was only half-a-dozen times.

We all looked up to [Lombardi], especially those of us who liked athletics. That was a great thrill. I didn't take advantage of it. Some of [the players] would come to Mass. Those who were Catholic. But he didn't require them to. One or two of the assistant coaches would be there. It was all very pleasant. The season hadn't started yet. It was summer camp.

[Fr. Burke] was a big tall man. Pleasant to be with. He was controversial in the sense that some of the rebel teachers on campus didn't like his decisions. I tried to stay out of that. Those of us who were dorm counselors—about half-a-dozen of us priests—we'd meet with him on Saturday afternoons. I recall the times he'd take me to Milwaukee to see a basketball game. I played a lot of golf with him.

Since [Burke] was a fundraiser for the college, he went out of his way to be nice to people even when he didn't agree with them. He went out of his way to be nice to the people who worked with him even when he didn't agree with them. He was gregarious. Fundraisers are that way. He'd take an interest in everything you did. He'd be generous to you.

They had different personalities. I understand Coach Lombardi could really lose his temper in a good way to motivate his players. One was Italian; the other was Irish. So they weren't that much alike. But there was mutual respect that grew into a friendship. [Fr. Burke] could control his temper. He didn't always agree with what was going on at the college, but he never lost his cool.

ABBOT JEROME TREMEL

Tremel was chairman of the mathematics department at St. Norbert from 1963 to 1969. A native of Luxemburg, he grew up in Green Bay and graduated from the old Central Catholic High School in 1947. Ordained in 1954, he's retired and living at St. Norbert Abbey.

I had very little contact with the Packers. Vince Lombardi served Mass for me a couple times. I have absolutely no interest in the Packers anyway, so I never paid much attention to them. They didn't get in my way; I didn't get in theirs.

[But] I went to visit Fr. [Luke] Dionne, who was dean of men, once in the dormitory and Vince came in and greeted us, then went down the hallway, went into a room and fined two of the players for watching television after curfew. This was in Sensenbrenner. I was living in Berne. It turned out there were three guys in the room and Vince never saw one of them. It was a black player. They had hit the lights right away. There were two in a room and [Lombardi] didn't realize there was a third one in there. We could hear him say, "Hey you two guys—whatever it was—it's 100 bucks apiece." He fined them, closed the door, backed away and came down the hallway past us and out he went. He lived in Victor McCormick [Hall]. A little while later, a third guy came out of that room and he happened to be black. He said, "That's the first time it ever paid to be black," because Vince didn't see him.

✤

Assistant Coaches and Staff

PAT PEPPLER

Peppler was hired by Lombardi as director of player personnel in 1963 and served in that capacity until Dan Devine appointed him assistant to the general manager in 1971. A native of Shorewood, Wis., Peppler spent more than 20 years as an administrator in the NFL. He was director of pro scouting for the Miami Dolphins under Don Shula from 1972 to 1974; general manager of the Atlanta Falcons from 1975 to 1976; assistant general manager of the Houston Oilers from 1977 to 1980; and director of football operations for most of his five years with the New Orleans Saints from 1981 to 1985. Peppler also was interim head coach of the Falcons for nine games in 1976.

I had a combination bedroom and office in Sensenbrenner Hall. It was on the first floor. It was like a corner room, so I could handle some of my business there and it also had a private place to sleep. Before I left for practice, I would stay behind and do some work on the telephone, talking to the league office or other clubs or the few agents that there were then or if there was anything to talk about with the food service people or the maids. I wasn't there very much, but I slept there.

We had a fairly big meeting room in the back corner of the basement toward the river. It probably held 60 or 70. It seemed more intimate than that, but before the cuts, there would be a fair share of people there.

The assistant coaches and I would switch off on bed checks. We'd each have a night or sometimes there'd be two of us. Most of the sneaking out was kind of subtle. The [players] wouldn't miss bed check. But after bed check, they could always have an excuse that they were going to the bathroom if they got caught on the way out. Curfew was at 11 o'clock and we'd conduct bed check right around that time. The guys who would sneak out would have some clever ways of doing things. I saw Max McGee one time when I was coming back to my room about 11:15, 11:30 sticking his head out of his room, looking around. He sees me and ducks back in. I was up for awhile reading or maybe talking to people on the West Coast. So a little later I went out of the room and there was Max taking another look. I think that time, after about three times, he gave up. But that doesn't tell how many times he looked and saw that the way was clear. There was a back entrance to the building. It was sort of an L-shaped building with a short end to the south. So a player could go in that entrance and go clear up to the third floor. Rumor was that [one player] didn't want to get caught out and get fined, so he would bring girls in. He'd get them in the back door and go up to third floor. He'd con the cleaning ladies into leaving a room open or having a key. We just used the first and second floors, and not all of the second floor. So the third floor was wide open, but there were mattresses on the beds. But most of the guys wanted to get out and go some place where it was comfortable.

Guys didn't jump out windows. Even the first floor was like halfway to a second floor. I don't know the extent of everything they did, but I'd be surprised if they jumped. They'd find another way. They knew the coaches and I weren't going to stay up all night.

The stories about [Max] McGee and [Paul] Hornung probably got exaggerated in some ways and underrated in others. I know for Hornung and McGee it was fun. They liked the sneaky part. And actually I think Lombardi got a kick out of the guys he thought were risk-takers.

I think the fine was somewhat arbitrary with Vince. One story (from 1964) you might be interested in is that I'd always go up to the office after the afternoon practice and get the waiver wire that had any trades or cutdowns that needed to be taken back to Sensenbrenner. I was there one day and Ruth McCloskey, who was Vince's secretary and book-keeper, called me in and said, "Pat, a fan sent this in. Take a look at this." She showed me where McGee had been arrested at 3:30 in the morning for speeding, somewhere between Appleton and St. Norbert. Ruth says, "What should I do?" Well I said, "Vince will just raise hell." I was halfway trying to protect the player, but I realized that wasn't fair to her, so I was pretty sure she was going to tell Vince. So when I went back out to camp, I got a hold of Max and said, "Max, the old man is going to find out that you snuck out and it was in the paper that you were arrested for speeding." Max says, "Pat, you know when I came up from Texas, I spent a few days down there with Fuzzy [Thurston]. I left some clothes there and just hadn't had a chance to get back down there. We got off early on Wednesday and I went down to pick up my clothes and was relaxing for a little bit and fell asleep. When I woke up it was about 3 in the morning and I headed back to camp." I said, "Max, you're not going to tell the old man that story are you?" He said, "Isn't it any good?" I said, "It's not worth a shit." Max was always blasé, so he wouldn't say thanks or anything like that. But Lombardi calls him on the carpet and when he got back, [McGee] just stuck his head in and said, "You saved me $250," and then kept on going. I kind of followed after him and said, "What happened?" He said the old man called him in and said, "Max, you snuck out." Max said, "Yes sir." Vince said, "That will cost you $250." The figures could have been higher. That doesn't really matter. But Vince said to Max, "It will cost you $250 and if you had lied to me it would have cost you $500." My experience was that Max was the primary guy as far as sneaking out.

All the coaches did the bed checks except Lombardi. Bill Austin and Norb Hecker [did] when they were there. The whole staff shared the thing. Nobody ever made a big fuss about it. Sometimes if you came in a little later [to check a room], a player might say, "You didn't think I'd be sneaking out did you?" They were kind of conning you. But it wasn't a major thing. It was half funny.

We didn't see much of Lombardi's temper out at St. Norbert. He may have raised hell at the meetings because he liked to keep them off balance. Things can get boring when you're with people as much as you are in training camp.

Fuzzy kind of ran the entertainment part at dinner. There were some pretty funny incidents. I even had to sing my first year there. I wasn't very good. I don't think we did it every night, but it was a fairly regular thing. The rookies had to sing, but we'd often get the best of the veterans up there. Elijah Pitts probably was the best. Travis Williams was good. He sang, *[Sittin' On] The Dock of the Bay*. That's where he was from [the San Francisco area]. Tommy Crutcher was a terrible singer, but he was funny as hell. They'd get him back and he'd do a poem about *Old Blue* that would crack everybody up. What Pittsie did was get two white guys and they sang, *We Three*. It was something like, "We three, we're all alone, living in a memory" and so forth. Then they cut one of the guys and they sang, "We two." Then they cut the other guy and Pittsie got up and sang, "We one." I think one of the white guys might have been Joe Scarpati. It seems to me he was in one of those things.

(Scarpati, who signed as a free agent, was in camp as a defensive back in 1964. Cut by the Packers, he was picked up by Philadelphia and played seven years in the NFL.)

Lombardi got a kick out of the singing. If they were bad, he got on Fuzzy. "He's terrible. Can't you do any better than that?" Lombardi wanted to put some pressure on them, too. If they were going to be pushed into entertainment, he wanted them to give it a good effort. Anybody who got up and did a good job or put some enthusiasm into it, he thought it was a little bit indicative of how they'd fit in on the club and all that. Sometimes, he'd be distracted and thinking about something else. But the entertainment went on.

[At] the 5 o'clock club, usually, you'd cut it off at two drinks. If you were going to drink, you could have a couple beers. Vince would usually have a couple Scotch and waters. Usually the first thing when we got there, we went through the waiver wire to see if there was anything interesting or anything that told us anything about our opponent. We talked football for that part of it. Then we'd joke around, talk about a variety of things. Lombardi would talk about some of the politicians. If we made any decisions, it would usually come after the player meetings. I'd be with the assistant coaches and Lombardi. There were only six of us. We'd meet like in the offensive room at Sensenbrenner. They had a big meeting room, and then one for the offense and one for the defense. Vince would ask—not every night—about the coaches' evaluations of the people at their positions. There was often some trade talk.

I thought St. Norbert was a good place for training camp. It was close enough that the players had some time where they could go home. And I think on Wednesday night, the coaches could go home. The facilities were fine. My setup was particularly good when I got that office. It was a good place to meet with players. I had to tell them when they had been cut. I'd usually grab them in the morning. We'd catch them in the dorm or after breakfast. It was partially because of the arrangements that had to be made for them to leave, so that was all resolved. We'd have to give them the bad news and tell them to bring their playbook. Then we would get them to the airport, make travel arrangements for them. We owed them a trip home.

I remember there was one kid who took it so bad that Vince let him stay another day. I think he was a fullback, a Big Ten type guy. He was so upset he begged Vince for another chance. Vince gave him another day and let the idea soak in on him, but he wasn't going to make it. Most of the time, you might tell them, "Maybe somebody else will pick you up or maybe it's time to move on."

BOB SCHNELKER

Schnelker was the Packers' receivers coach during Lombardi's final two seasons as head coach and during the year Lombardi served as general manager. Schnelker played tight end for the New York Giants in the 1950s when Lombardi ran the offense. After Lombardi left the Packers following the 1968 season, Schnelker was put in charge of the team's passing game and remained in that post through 1971. He returned to the Packers in 1982 and was their offensive coordinator for another four seasons. In all, Schnelker spent 28 years as an assistant coach in the NFL with seven different teams.

St. Norbert was very limited. We had to live in those dorms out there and then take a bus all the way over to the practice field. The bus rides were the worst. The coaches would drive their own cars, but the players had to ride the buses from St. Norbert to the stadium. The players hated it, but there was no other way to do it. And they didn't want them driving their cars because somebody might have an accident or something.

Other teams used colleges, but the practice fields were right there. With St. Norbert, you had the damn bus ride. St. Norbert was unusual because of all the driving you had to do to sleep and eat, and go to practice. I'm surprised they're still there.

The assistant coaches all stayed at the dorms. Vince stayed, too. Not all the time. I'm pretty sure of that. I think his room was in the other dorm. I know he'd stay out there because we'd go out for a beer, come back and Vince might be walking around.

We had our meetings out there. All the player meetings were out there. Just the practices were at the stadium. We'd start out with a team meeting. Vince always liked a team meeting. From there, we'd break up into our individual groups. I'd take the receivers.

As long as people did what they were supposed to do, the meetings went pretty well. If there were mental mistakes, Vince would get upset. Physical mistakes he understood. He didn't blow off that much when things went right. But if practice didn't go right, he'd get upset. He was known for that: blowing up at guys who did something wrong. And it didn't matter who it was. He didn't play favorites like I've seen other head coaches do.

They filmed the practice and we'd go over that. We had no meeting rooms at the stadium until they remodeled. It could get pretty fierce if somebody did something wrong. If somebody knew they did something wrong and knew it was coming up on film, they'd be shrinking back in their chairs.

In the position meetings, you'd go over any mistakes that were made that day. Or maybe something new was put in. You refined things that you did. A lot depended on how good a guys you had. The guys I had were mostly veterans: McGee, Boyd Dowler, Carroll Dale.

They were all pretty good players, smart players. So I didn't have a whole lot of mistakes to go over.

Some nights the team meeting wouldn't be very long at all. You'd maybe just go over what was going to happen the next day. Or if there were problems, you might talk about those. But the team meetings weren't that long unless we were getting near game time. But, heck, in those days, we used to go to training camp for weeks and weeks and weeks. Now, some of them go in for maybe 10 days before they play a game.

The first meeting would start, I suppose, at 7 o'clock [at night] and we'd be out of there by 8:30, quarter-to-nine. Vince always said, "Don't keep them too long. Get done what you have to get done, but don't keep them there forever."

[Lombardi] had a great speaking voice. He was smart. He had studied to be a lawyer. So he knew words. He could get up there and say the right things, and it wouldn't take forever to do it. He knew what to say and when to say it and when the players needed it.

After that, then there was curfew. I think some of the older guys went out and drank beer for awhile. Maybe for some of the younger ones, it was new for them and they went to bed. They were pretty tired. The coaches went to different places, too. There was a place south, Wrightstown. We'd go down there. There was a nice bar right downtown. Most of the guys went. Hawgie [Dave Hanner] was one. Phil [Bengtson] was older. He and Lombardi were together all the time. After meetings, you'd see them walking around. Then maybe they'd both go home. Ray Wietecha was a beer drinker. That's how Jerry Burns and I became good friends. When he became head coach [of the Vikings], I became his offensive coordinator. We were hired by Lombardi the same day. Pat Peppler went [out with the coaches].

But each night one of the assistant coaches was in charge of checking the rooms. So [if it was your night], you had to stay in. In those days, there were maybe five, six, seven coaches. So at least once a week, you were going to have bed check. You had to stay in in case something came up, if somebody got sick or something. So you couldn't go out and drink beers with the guys.

Guys would sneak out sometimes. We had done it as players. So if we weren't the guy who had to check them in, we didn't worry about it. Let the guy checking them in worry about it. We'd stay out until after curfew. We didn't get someplace until about 10 o'clock. So if you had a couple beers, it would be after curfew.

Each of us had a room—a private room—but it wasn't fancy. It seemed like an old place even then. We had rooms on the first floor. I can remember looking out my window sometimes and seeing Vince walk by. Either he was going home or going out for some fresh air.

We'd wear our coaching clothes [on the campus]. That way we didn't have any laundry to worry about. I think the school must have done it. We had fresh clothes. The equipment guys would bring it right to the dorm. They knew who was whose. It was marked and you always got the same stuff. So they must have done it right at the school. They must have had a laundromat there. Once in awhile, we'd sneak home. But that was your job and you knew that. And we did get some relaxation when everybody was done for the day and we'd go out for a couple hours.

The 5 o'clock club was a fun thing. Vince had a lot of visitors. A lot of guys from New York would come and stay a few days—buddies of his. We got to know those guys. Vince was at his best with those guys. Football was forgotten. That was the relaxation part of the day. We'd talk about the topic of the day, maybe things that happened in practice, funny things or bad things. [We'd talk about] things that were going on in that day and age, either in the world or in Green Bay. It was a nice big room. So Vince and his buddies would be over this way and the coaches over this way.

I was with the Giants when Vince was the coach there and he brought that [the 5 o'clock club] from the Giants. I think the Giants started it. Believe it or not, we went to Salem, Oregon, for training camp for about five years. And we went to Winooski, Vermont, one year. Bear Mountain. What happened—this was the Fifties—was that the Yankees were always in the World Series. So we couldn't use Yankee Stadium to practice. That's when we'd go to Bear Mountain. So we were up there three, four, five years in a row. Vince was offensive coach then. I don't know who started it with the Giants. I would assume it was Jack Mara,

Wellington's older brother. He was the president of the club. I was a player. We knew there was a 5 o'clock club, but we didn't know what it was. We just knew the coaches went there. But that was true. Vince brought it from the Giants to Green Bay. He never put a limit on what you could do. You had snacks there. And then you'd go right from there to dinner. Good meals. Always good food. And plenty of it.

BILL AUSTIN

Austin, the last survivor from Lombardi's original staff in Green Bay, served as offensive line coach from 1959 to 1964. Lombardi's original staff included four coaches: Austin, offensive backfield coach Red Cochran, defensive line coach Phil Bengtson and defensive backfield coach Norb Hecker. Austin played guard for the New York Giants for seven years, including the time when Lombardi was an assistant coach with them. Austin also served as line coach during Lombardi's one year as head coach of the Washington Redskins and then succeeded him as head coach in 1970 following Lombardi's death. In addition to his one year as head coach of the Redskins, Austin also was head coach of the Pittsburgh Steelers from 1966 to 1968.

I think they were a bunch of undisciplined players [in 1958] and the goal was to get some discipline. We had some good personnel and we wanted [them to develop] a good attitude so that they could win. The talent was there. Jimmy Taylor was in his second year. Hornung. The tight ends, whether it was the Michigan guy [Ron Kramer] or [Gary] Knafelc. And the two guards were there. We just had to have more discipline.

As a player, I had been though a number of years with Lombardi when he was an assistant coach. Of course, he ran the offense with the Giants. I didn't think the training camp was that tough. We had to find out what each player could do. And in Lombardi's own way, he put the pressure on them to perform. And if you couldn't perform, you were gone.

[Lombardi] was no different in training camp than in league play. But I believe he liked to put pressure on and see if the player cracked. He'd put the pressure on them in practice, not meetings.

When he'd get that chalk in his hand and started putting diagrams on the blackboard [at meetings], you better remember what he wrote up there if you were a player. He just came across a little stronger than most people I coached with.

I didn't think [putting in the Lombardi sweep was complicated] because I was an offensive guard who played for him when he was offensive coordinator with the New York Giants. So I ran those Fuzzy Thurston and Jerry Kramer blocking patterns. [Lombardi] would break a few pieces of chalk at the board. But that was the way he coached.

JERRY BURNS

Burns was defensive backfield coach of the Packers from 1966 to 1967. After Burns left Green Bay, he became offensive coordinator of the Minnesota Vikings under Bud Grant. Burns held that position from 1968 to 1985 and then became head coach of the Vikings. In his six years as head coach of the Vikings, from 1986 to 1991, he compiled a 55-46 record.

All I know [St. Norbert] was a nice place and we were treated great. I was with Phil Bengtson and Hawg Hanner and the defense, other than the meetings that were more team oriented. But when we broke up, the offense went with Lombardi and the defense went with Bengtson.

In all my years of coaching in the National Football League, I never saw any better a defensive man than Phil Bengtson. Very smart and convinced that the things we were doing were right. He sold everybody on his 4-3 scheme and, as a consequence, the defense was very strong. He was a great guy. Easygoing and more player-oriented than Lombardi. Lombardi was like a drill sergeant, while Bengtson had a little more intimate relationship [with his players]. I'm not being critical of Lombardi. I'm just telling you the relationship of the offensive players with Lombardi and the defensive players with Phil Bengtson was different. Bengtson was a genius as a defensive coordinator.

The guys I remember were Jim Taylor, Paul Hornung, Ray Nitschke, Fuzzy Thurston, Max McGee. He was always a fun guy to be around.

They were all pretty well disciplined, but they had a little fun with you and kidded you about this or that. They were all good guys and the discipline Lombardi expected on the field, he expected when we were eating dinner, bed checks, whatever. Now, they have anywhere from 18 to 22, 23 coaches. On offense, we had three guys and Lombardi; and on defense, there were just three of us: Hawg Hanner, myself and Bengtson.

[Lombardi] was in a different vein than the other coaches. Sometimes at the 5 o'clock club you'd meet, but he also was the general manager. He was offensive coordinator. He was on a 24-hour schedule and he was a busy guy. I don't think we avoided him, [but] he was maybe on a little tighter schedule than the other coaches.

I remember the [5 o'clock club] always broke up at five or 10 [minutes] to 6, and we got to the chow line on time. The 5 o'clock club with Green Bay was almost like a responsibility to be there. With other teams, it was just an opportunity to go have a bottle of beer and relax a little. Basically, Lombardi was there and sometimes he wanted to talk about this or talk about that. So you made yourself available. Most everybody was there unless they had a reasonable excuse.

CHUCK LANE

Lane was 23 years old when Lombardi hired him as publicity director in 1966. Lane's title was changed to director of public relations a year later and he held that position through the 1979 season, except for a year off in 1974 when he went to work for Bart Starr. Lane is currently director of incentive travel and public relations for Humana. Prior to joining the Packers, Lane earned seven letters in football and baseball at Washington and Lee University, and did promotional work for the Harlem Globetrotters.

I came [to Green Bay] in March 1966, and had three, four months working with [Lombardi before camp started]. So I knew him and I would honestly say feared him. He inspired a great deal of respect, but also there was that fear factor that kept you on your toes. Anybody who said they weren't afraid of him, I think was lying. We all were.

I had most of my communication with him, most of my daily contact with him over at Lambeau Field during the day and tried to stay away from him as best I could in the evening. He had his 5 o'clock club and that was where I had most of my contact with him at St. Norbert. Any writers or broadcasters or whomever wanted access to him, I'd try to set that up in advance so the interview could happen during the 5 to 6 o'clock hour. It was a thing he brought with him to Green Bay from the New York Giants. I thought it was a pretty good idea because it was a much more relaxed atmosphere. The coach would mix himself a Scotch or grab a beer and sit down in a very casual situation. His assistant coaches would always be there. It was my role to make sure the refrigerator was stocked, pick up the hors d'oeuvres from over in the Sensenbrenner cafeteria—cheese and crackers, things like that.

The 5 o'clock club was Monday through Friday. It was really a relaxed discussion of things political, social. It didn't always happen to be football. In fact, I don't think I ever heard anybody discuss in great measure any personnel decisions or strategic things. I think it was [Lombardi's] one hour of the day where he could really relax for a little bit. What he'd do was meet with the media after practice. Once the players were dismissed, he'd stand around the tower out there on the practice field on Oneida Street and answer questions with the media. You know it was amazing that our media exposure was so limited in those days. You had two guys from Milwaukee, one guy from Green Bay. Every once in awhile you'd get somebody from AP or UPI. But, by and large, very seldom would we get anybody else. Maybe Tex Maule from Sports Illustrated would come in or a guy from Sport magazine. For the playoff games every year, we'd get a whole gaggle of those people. But during training camp there was very few media.

Fr. Burke would be there periodically. He was a real gentleman. Lombardi liked him a lot. I think he confided in him a great deal. With Lombardi's background and everything, I think that was a traditional thing to have friends in the priesthood. Fr. Burke would travel with us to away games on occasion.

Tex Maule was superb. I thought he was one of the classiest guys I ever met. We used to go out to dinner periodically. Bill Heinz would stop by periodically. You'd get an occasional New York writer who knew Lombardi. Jimmy Breslin was another one who stopped out on occasion. He was New York, Irish, a tremendous character, unique speaking style. The 5 o'clock club was when these guys had access to [Lombardi]. I don't think he ever stonewalled me when I asked him if he would have time for an interview out there. [Lombardi] gave them, quite frankly, preferred treatment, access. Those were his roots. Those were the people he was comfortable with. How do I say this? I don't know if [Lombardi] had a great deal of respect for the local writers he saw and read on a daily basis. He was more respectful of the Eastern writers than he was the local writers. He used to treat Lee [Remmel] and Art [Daley] [both of the Press-Gazette] just terribly. And he'd mistreat them in front of other writers. He'd just abuse them.

[Lombardi's] in-law would be out there every summer. That was just a circus. Jim Lawlor. I think he was like a cousin to Marie. I think maybe he played with Lombardi. He might have played with him at Fordham. Big, tall. He was a John Wayne type of guy. Rawboned. He was a parole officer in New York or New Jersey and he used to give Coach Lombardi the hardest time. He was putting him on all the time. The rest of us couldn't believe he could get away with this. Lombardi loved him. Lawlor was a character, irreverent as hell. Everybody else was kissing the coach's backside and this Lawlor was taking a piece of skin off him every time he could. He'd be there every summer. He'd be here for a week or so. He'd drive over to practice with the coach and be there all day. He'd hang around. He was wonderful company.

(Lawlor had been Lombardi's roommate at Fordham, and also was Marie Lombardi's first cousin.)

Everybody had a few at the 5 o'clock club. Beer, wine. Coach always had a Scotch or two. Phil [Bengtson] always had a large glass of bourbon filled right to the top. I think people got a little bit loose, but I never saw anybody get really drunk. What was really funny was that Schnelker and Burns used to have a thing going and they were just like little mischievous boys. They'd sneak into the refrigerator—we'd always have three, four varieties of beer—and pick up a can of beer, shake the hell out of it and put it back in there. It was like having a landmine in there. Nobody knew when it was going to go off. But they'd laugh like hell when somebody came out of there all festooned with a beer that spewed on them.

Nobody laughed any harder at stuff than Coach Lombardi and especially at his own jokes. He had one of the most infectious laughs in the world. You couldn't help but laugh along with him.

We only had an hour for the 5 o'clock club and it was always breakneck to leave the practice field and get over there. So very seldom did the 5 o'clock club start right at 5. But, by gosh, you were out of there by 6. It was Lombardi time and he'd get over to the food line and make sure nobody overstayed their time at Buck's and the other places the players were going at that time.

Dinner was pretty laid back. We'd always sit in the same area as the coach. The rookies would have to get up and sing. I remember having to do that myself. I was terrified, but it was part of the initiation. If you were going to be part of the team, this is what you did. You could just pick a song. [Lombardi] always seemed to be able to turn it on and turn it off. You could tell when he was out of sorts. But, by and large, at dinner he'd be loosened up after a drink or two. He'd laugh like hell [during the singing]. It probably enabled him to get a feel for the young guys. See how a guy reacted and how his teammates reacted to him. I don't remember him ever saying, "That guy is terrible," or "Get him out of here." I think virtually all pro teams in those days did that sort of thing. But I never saw any malicious hazing with the Packers, which I've heard about with other teams, where rookies had to wait on veterans, or wait for the veterans to be seated.

[The players] would go over and slam a lot of beer on their stops before they got over [to dinner]. There'd be a lot of giggling and grab-assing. You could tell they'd had a few. But [Lombardi] pretty much ignored it. It was like he knew boys were going to be boys.

Fuzzy would get up and sing *He's Got the Whole World in His Hands*. He was kind of the Mitch Miller of the group. He'd get the crowd going. And Lombardi loved it. Fuz would kind of play to him, "We've got the greatest coach in the land, greatest quarterback, greatest running backs, greatest defense." Fuz just loved to hear himself.

The food was fantastic. Big, steamship rounds of beef and there'd be a guy over there with a carving knife whacking big chunks of that. They'd have beef, ham, chicken, a little of everything. You name it, it was there.

After the intra-squad and home preseason games, [Lombardi] would always have an open house or reception for players, wives, families, staff. It was in the dining hall. Coach was very jovial. He was absolutely a great host. He'd wander around from table to table, chat with the wives, rough up the hair of the kids. He was superb. And, frankly, he was pretty steady—win, lose or draw. In fact, a lot of people said he was better after having lost a game than after winning ugly. That's when he'd really get pissed off.

Marie was wonderful, too. David Maraniss' book dealt with her excessive drinking, but I never saw that in the three years I was around her. I never saw a hint of her having too much to drink. She was a great hostess, too. She was always one to stand up for the players. If he was hard on a player, she'd always stand up for them and tell him he was being a pain in the ass. I really enjoyed her. She was as strong a personality as he was. There were some historic arguments between the two and she'd never back down. I'd see that like on a bus or something like that.

I think my second year [1967] I lived at St. Norbert. I was between apartments and to save a little bit of rent I stayed in the dorm. I was rooming with Dave Hanner. He contended that he roomed with my suitcase. But I never heard a man snore like that in my life. I couldn't sleep. I'd look over at him and Dave would be covered with just a sheet. You don't realize how big a man he was. He was covered with this white sheet and when he was breathing, the sheet would almost rise and fall. It looked like a leaf pile. My gosh! Did he make sounds. Sometimes I'd sneak in really late with half a package on just so I could get some sleep. But, by and large, I just didn't bother to come back.

The assistant coaches had to do the curfew thing. I think two of them would do it each night. But those guys probably slipped away for a few cocktails themselves after they were done or go home for awhile. I think curfew was 11. I think all the assistants had rooms there. Whether they all stayed there every night, I don't know. There was the story about finding McGee and Hornung in bed. I don't know if that was true or not. A lot of those stories have been embellished. I think it was seldom that the coaches checked a second time. By and large, I think they were eager to get the hell out of the [dorm] themselves. I was gone until the hours of 11 or 12, so I don't really have any idea. I'd sneak in, tiptoe in and climb into bed. I don't think [a lot of players broke curfew]. In Green Bay, people could call Lombardi and say so-and-so was out. Nobody can hide in this town. The dorms were a pretty orderly place. Some of that stuff might have been going on, but I didn't see it.

There'd be kids all over the place [on campus]. And I never saw a more respectful group of players and fans. There'd be a lot of kids sitting around with slips of paper. A lot of times the little guys were just terrified and somebody like Ray [Nitschke] would go over and say, "Aren't you going to ask me for my autograph?" The kids were great and I never saw a player turn a kid down for an autograph.

AL TREML

Treml started doing film work for the Packers on a part-time basis in 1964 and became the team's first full-time film director in 1967. He held that position for 34 years and was inducted into the Packer Hall of Fame in 2008 as a contributor. A native of Green Bay, Treml graduated from the old Central Catholic High School in 1955.

I went out [to St. Norbert] for meals and the 5 o'clock club. I didn't stay out there. What I'd do is after practice, I'd go down to WBAY and process the film, then I'd take it out there. Depending on what time practice got over and how much filming we had would determine what time I'd get there. Sometimes I would get there to go to the 5 o'clock club. Other times I'd get there toward the end of meal time. Sometimes, it would be just prior to the meeting. But I would go out there every day that we practiced. But back then they didn't shoot practice as much as now.

If there were evening meetings, I'd go home. At that time, it was simply overhead projections and screens. That was all the equipment we had [at St. Norbert]. All [the coaches] would have to do is show it and they had projectors where they could run the film back and forth. The film would be in different reels. I'd have the team portion on one reel, say seven-on-seven on another reel and short-yardage and goal-line on another. The defense could be in one room looking at some, the offense in another and they could trade them back and forth.

I always thought [the 5 o'clock club] was a really neat time. It was the press and coaching staff pretty much, and everybody was at ease. [Lombardi] used to be many times more relaxed than you'd ever see him and enjoying himself. Then at a certain time, he'd look at his watch and say, "Time to go." And that was the end of the 5 o'clock club that day.

Memories [of dinner] would be the singing of the rookies. Each year a member of the team was assigned the singing duties. A veteran. In 1967, my first year full time, Willie Wood was chairman of the singing. He made sure they had enough people singing. He'd call on different people. He even called on me. Everybody had to sing sooner or later. I sang, *Five Foot Two, Eyes of Blue*. Not very well. Everybody was laughing. I don't know how the rookie players felt, but I felt very relieved when I was done with my singing. For me, it was just a one-time thing. Some of the players they'd call on more often, especially the No. 1 and 2 draft choices. Some were pretty good. Some would belt it out and have a good time. Others would sing their school song and not be very good.

CHAPTER 4

✣

The Players (Part 1)

BART STARR

A lowly 17th-round draft pick in 1956, Starr showed enough promise to make the Packers' roster, but he foundered over the next three seasons. In 1959, Vince Lombardi's first as coach, Starr started the final five games and led the Packers to victory in four of them. He won the job outright in the sixth game of the 1960 season and led the Packers into the NFL championship game that year and then to five titles over the next seven years, including the first two Super Bowls. Starr was inducted into the Pro Football Hall of Fame in 1977. He also served as the Packers' head coach from 1975 to 1983.

I thought it was an ideal situation that the Packers and St. Norbert worked out during the training camp period. We could be housed there, hold our meetings there. We spent the evenings there. I thought it was a perfect fit because of the convenience, the closeness, the friendliness of everyone associated with the college. It was just a very enjoyable experience. The setting at St. Norbert and in De Pere was very practical. We couldn't have been in a better environment. You could walk around a little bit, meet people, say hello to them.

I enjoyed meeting people. My father had stressed when we moved around—my father was a career military man—that you could be friendly to people regardless of age. That you could be sociable, kind,

63

generous. So when you had an opportunity to be [around the young fans on campus], you'd try to help them anyway you could: Answer questions, be cordial about signing autographs. It was fun.

We learned a great deal [in Lombardi's first year]. He simplified the terminology, which had been a lot of gobbledygook stuff. He reduced the terminology that was necessary to call plays and those types of things. You could see from the very first meeting that this man was extremely well-organized and well-prepared. [Meetings] were always relatively short. I think he felt if he could keep it as simple as possible, it would be much more appealing for the players. Plus, I think he felt he could maintain discipline by being narrowly focused and speaking in that fashion.

In those days, he didn't have an offensive coordinator, so [Lombardi] basically coached the offense. He was always uniquely well prepared. He taught well. Anytime we had a meeting, I could hardly wait to go to the next [one] because I knew he'd be conducting it. He was just an outstanding teacher and coach.

Mostly, [I roomed] with Henry Jordan. Henry Jordan had a great sense of humor. It was super fun rooming with a guy like that. He was a great guy. Most of the time when we went back [to the room], we just went to bed. But it was a good roommate-teammate package. We had some very good discussions. [And] we were a little more subdued than [Paul Hornung and Max McGee]. [But Lombardi] loved those guys because even though they didn't like curfew, they never embarrassed themselves or the team. So Coach Lombardi turned his head and fined the heck out of them. The next morning at practice, no one was sharper, no one was more committed or prepared than those two guys. Many of us always figured that when we had our team party at the end of the year, their fines paid for our party.

In the afternoon, when we wanted to get a beer before the meetings, we'd go over to a nice pub in East De Pere. Just over the bridge and to the right. They treated us very well and very privately. It was just a way for us to get away for a few minutes. During training camp, we went over there frequently.

(The pub he was referring to was Century Bowling Lanes and Bar, located at 132 S. Broadway St.)

FORREST GREGG

In his book Run to Daylight, *Lombardi called Gregg "the finest player I ever coached." An offensive tackle, Gregg joined the Packers in 1956 as a second-round draft pick, went into service for a year, then returned in 1958 and played through 1970. He played in 187 consecutive games for the Packers, the second longest streak in club history to Brett Favre. Gregg was inducted into the Pro Football Hall of Fame in 1977. He also served as the Packers' head coach from 1984 to 1987.*

I went [to St. Norbert] from 1958 until 1970, then came back there when I was coaching at Green Bay. St. Norbert had good facilities. The cafeteria was great. It had everything you needed: meeting rooms, everything for a training camp.

I had heard about [Lombardi] during the off-season [of 1959]. I didn't have any idea as to who he was or what he was like. I lived in Dallas during the off-season and [Southern Methodist University] had some kind of function. I ran into a friend of mine and he said, "So you all got a new coach in Green Bay." I said, "Yeah, a guy named Vince Lombardi." He said, "Do you know anything about him?" I said, "Absolutely not. I don't know a thing about him. Do you?" He said, "Yeah, he's a real bastard."

It was a guy named Don "Tiny" Goss. Tiny was at SMU when I was there. He was drafted by the Cleveland Browns and played one year. I think he was in Cleveland in 1956 and '57, then he [went to] the Giants, I think in '58. I don't know for how long, but it was long enough to figure out what Vince was.

When it came time to go to training camp John Symank, a defensive back who lived in Arlington, and I rode up to Green Bay together. The second night, we got as far as Milwaukee and we decided we'd stop, have dinner and go into camp the next day. In the meantime, I said, "John, why don't we call Dave Hanner and see what's going on, just in case we're missing something?" So we call Dave up and said, "How is it going?" He says, "Whew-eee!" I said, "What do you mean?"

He said, "I've already been to the hospital twice from heat exhaustion. This training camp is like nothing you could ever dream of," as far as the past is concerned. John and I put our heads together and we said, "We won't have any chance of making this team. We better get up to Green Bay." We checked out of the hotel, jumped in the car and got to [St. Norbert] about midnight or a little after.

There was a camp boy there checking people into the rooms. I told the guy, "We kind of got in late. John and I are going to sleep in, and we'll come and meet Coach Lombardi at lunch." The guy kind of smiled and said, "OK." At 6:45, some guy was beating on our door. "Get out here." We said, "We're sleeping in." "Coach Lombardi wants to see you guys at the cafeteria as soon as you get there." We jumped up, put on our clothes and took off over to the cafeteria.

I'll never forget meeting him. The boy took us over and told Coach Lombardi who we were. My first impression was that he was kind of short, not a real big guy, but blocky. Had a real nice smile. I shook hands with him and he had a real firm handshake. I thought, "Well, this seems like a pretty good guy." He says, "Glad you guys came in a little early. We've got a lot of work to do. I'll see you at practice." That was the introduction to him.

At the first practice, we did about 45, 50 grass drills. Up-downs, we called them. It seemed like 100. I don't know how many it was, but my tongue was hanging out. We got through the grass drills, then we started on agility drills and then we broke down further from there and the offensive line went over to its corner of the practice field. We were going over some plays, doing some technique drills. Bill Austin was our line coach. All of a sudden, I hear this screaming. It was like a rabid dog. I look over and Max McGee was walking back to the huddle. Lombardi was behind him, "Mister! We don't walk anywhere here! We run wherever we go! When you run out for a pass pattern, you run back to the huddle! You don't walk back to the huddle!" The more [Lombardi] talked the faster Max got.

[When Lombardi introduced the sweep], he drew this play up on the board. He said, "This is the play we've got to learn to execute. This play has everything to do with our total offense. We pass from the same formation. We run off tackle from the same formation. We run short traps, long traps, a dive from that formation. Everything has the same look from this beginning." He went through everything: how the guards pulled and led the play and what they would be looking for; the tight end's block; the split receiver's block; tackles, running backs, everybody. He said, "We will make this play work." And we did.

That wasn't the first meeting. The rookies were still the main source of attention. But I think it was the first full offensive meeting after everybody reported. It was football. It wasn't anything I hadn't seen before. [But] he was definite about it and I figured I better learn what I was supposed to do and figure out how to get it done. That was kind of how everybody looked at it.

The first two years I played pro ball, which was '56 and '58, I never thought I was in good enough condition to play my best the whole game. After a couple weeks in [Lombardi's first] training camp, I knew I was going to be ready to play. I just hoped I'd get an opportunity. I could just tell by the mood of the players that we were going to get better as a football team. I didn't know how good we were going to be. I had no way of knowing that we were going to be the team of the Sixties. But it was obvious that things were going to be different. You know Henry Jordan made that joke about how [Lombardi] treated us all the same, like dogs? Well, he did. He said several times and it really hit home with me, "I'll paint you all with the same brush. The rules are for everybody, not just one guy. There's no one guy greater than this football team." I liked that type of philosophy and I related to it.

I remember we played the Bears in Milwaukee that first season in preseason. They ran a screen pass on us and that big fullback, [Rick] Casares, scored on us and beat us. We were looking at film two days later at St. Norbert. [Lombardi] stopped the film and said, "I want to show you a ballplayer." I had no idea what he was talking about. We ran a trap play and my assignment was to release inside the defensive end, go across and hit the middle linebacker. It wasn't Bill George, I can tell you that right now. It was some rookie middle linebacker and I caught him looking. I knocked him on the ground and then jumped on top of him. [Lombardi] ran that play three, four times and my heart was beating so fast, I thought I was going to pass out. That was the first time he ever said anything really [nice] about me. What he did was—he expected that from me every game. He set the standard.

(George played middle linebacker for the Bears from 1952 to 1965 and was inducted into the Pro Football Hall of Fame in 1974.)

GARY KNAFELC

Knafelc started at tight end for the Packers in Lombardi's first two seasons after playing wide receiver earlier in his career. In all, Knafelc played for the Packers from 1954 to 1962. He played one game for the Chicago Cardinals before joining the Packers as a free agent and one year for the San Francisco 49ers at the end of his career. He was inducted into the Packers Hall of Fame in 1976.

I remember how tough that [first] camp was. That was the first time we had a nutcracker drill, the up-down drills. He just killed us all. We had our [first] meeting in the old Quonset hut. I remember how intense he was: "If you don't hustle here, you won't be here." The first speech was not that long as I recall. It was very precise as to what he expected. And if you didn't want to play for him, the way he wanted you to play, you weren't going to be playing with the Green Bay Packers. It was as simple as that. Bart and I were talking, "Holy mackerel!" We had Scooter McLean for a coach. We said there's going to be tremendous change here. But both of us said, "We're going to be a winner with this guy." We all knew it. Scooter McLean had played poker with guys on Saturday nights on away trips before the games and he lost money to Max. Can you imagine that? In training camp we had to be in at 10:30 or something like that, but nobody ever checked your room before Lombardi came. Then the [assistant] coaches checked them all week and [Lombardi] checked them on Friday night. Just on Friday night.

I'm sure you heard the story about Hornung and McGee pulling the beds together. On a Friday night, they knew it was going to be

Coach Lombardi. So he knocked on their room and they had pulled their two twin beds together. They were naked and when [Lombardi] opened the door, they were laying in bed hugging each other. He closed the door and left. That's definitely a true story.

[Starr] was my roommate. We were both very intense about trying to make the ballclub [that first year]. Bart wasn't the fair-haired boy and neither was I. Coach Lombardi had brought in Lamar McHan. Bart was a second-stringer.

During training camp, Ron Kramer, Steve Meilinger and I were fighting for the tight end position. The week before the opener, we broke camp at St. Norbert and Coach Lombardi took us all down to St. John's Academy. That was with our wives, our kids, everybody. The whole week we trained down there. We had a big scrimmage Thursday night before we broke camp. He brought us [the tight ends] all together and said, "Line up." The Packer sweep to the right side was "Red White 49." He called that and said, "Knafelc get in at tight end." I got in at tight end. He said the only ones live are the ball-carrier, linebacker and off-guard. The tight end splits nine feet from the tackle. That's a long way. If the linebacker in front of you comes down the line, you must cut him off before he makes penetration or he'll knock the guards off. If he comes straight up the field, you stop him and turn him, and drive him to the outside because as soon as the ball is snapped the off-guard and the running back look at the tight end. If they see his numbers they go inside. If they don't see his numbers they go outside.

The whole thing is predicated on the block of the tight end. So Lombardi stood behind me where I couldn't see him. He'd point to the linebacker in front of me to come down the line or come straight. The first one was Dan Currie and I blocked him for about 10 plays. Then he put Bubba [Bill Forester] over there and I blocked him for about 10 plays. Then he put [Ray] Nitschke in. I'm just worn out. All that time, [Lombardi] is chewing my ass out: "Move your feet, get your legs," all that kind of crap. In fact, my sons were watching practice. The last one, I'm beat up, my legs are shaking. I'm exhausted. I'm standing there by Coach Lombardi worn out and said real quietly,

"Even Nitschke knows it's a run, coach." He looked at me, didn't say anything. "Everybody in." My little son, my five-year old Guy, looked at me and said, "Dad, I still love you." The next day at breakfast, we're breaking camp and I'm sitting with my wife and two sons. I can see Coach Lombardi coming toward our table. I told my wife, "Coach Lombardi is coming to our table. He's going to cut me." She said, "He wouldn't cut you." He stops at the table, looks at me and says, "You're going to start Sunday." And then he walked away. That's what he would do. In front of the whole team, he'd chew your ass out and make you feel like you were nothing. Then in front of my whole family that's how I learned I was starting.

I was always the first one to line up in the nutcracker drill. I wanted to get it over with. Bart and I were walking after our evening meal [once] and Coach Lombardi was walking behind us. I said, "Let's cross the street." He crossed the street, too. I said, "Ohhh, shit." I thought he was going to cut me. He walked up to me—we were walking kind of fast because I didn't want to talk to him—and he said, "Gary." I said, "Yes, Coach." He said, "You had some pretty good blocks today." I said, "Well, Coach, fear does wonderful things." He kind of laughed and kept on going.

You never knew what to expect [that first year] and he surprised you every day. Our schedule was: You get out on the field and run a lap first. Then the receivers would get together with the quarterbacks and run patterns. You'd warm up that way. Then he'd bring us altogether and we'd do our up-down drills. He'd stand right in front and watch everybody. Up and down, and he'd make sure nobody tried to cheat and that kind of stuff. Then we'd start our scrimmage. We figured after the up-down drills, the scrimmages were downhill. We had never had that kind of stuff before. But I'll tell you, by the fourth quarter, we were in such great shape that we all knew if the game was close there was no way we were going to lose it. We were always in better shape than anybody we ever played.

On edge? Well, sure. You didn't know if you were going to be there or not. How could you not be on edge [that first year]? He was cutting guys right and left. He already traded Bill Howton the first time he was in town and he was by far our best player. He cut Jerry Helluin. He cut Babe Parilli. Al Carmichael.

(Within three months after being named coach, Lombardi traded end Billy Howton to the Cleveland Browns for defensive end Bill Quinlan and halfback Lew Carpenter. Howton had been first-team all-pro two years earlier and had led the Packers in receptions six of the previous seven seasons, but had a reputation for being a clubhouse lawyer.)

On the field, [Lombardi] criticized you constantly. He chewed my ass out all the time. Some guys he didn't. I figure he knew he could do it with me and he sure did, but it made me a hell of a lot better ballplayer. I was a wide receiver for five years. I never played tight end before.

The meetings [in 1959] were tough because you had to be prepared. He'd call you up to the blackboard, any time and indiscriminately, and he'd give you three offensive plays against three defensive plays and you'd have to diagram what everybody did against those defenses. You were not going to be embarrassed when you went up there. So you studied that playbook. That was one reason why our offense was so good. Everyone knew what everybody was supposed to do all the time. He did that every year. The first year we had never done it before. It was really a shock. But his system was such that after the first year, you didn't have any problems. I could still diagram all the plays. But we had several guys who got up there and [couldn't do it] and got their ass chewed and were told to sit down. But they weren't around after that.

All of us were underweight. I was only 215 pounds. Dave [Hanner] was in the hospital with heat prostration. We couldn't have water on the field. That's how dumb it was. It was the up-down drills. I was always in the front row. It wasn't that I wanted him to see me. But he'd stand sometimes next to me, so he wouldn't be looking at me; he'd be looking at the guys behind and I could cheat a little.

[Hanner] was a good football player. He played a long time. It was amazing. David was the kind of guy who looked puffy and fat. But within about three centimeters of that fat he was like concrete. It was like hitting a post. He was hard as a rock, but he looked fat and flabby. And real blond, white face. He would get red as a beet. He just passed out that time and they had to take him to the hospital. It was those up-down drills. We thought he was dead. It was so hot out there and you couldn't have any water. And that was hard work.

There was a restaurant where we'd go and get a hamburger and milk shake at night. Bart and I stopped there all the time. If you came over the bridge, it was the [third] building on the left. We'd go for a walk just to get out of the place and we'd stop by there.

(The restaurant was the Nicolet Dairy Bar, located at 313 Main Ave. in West De Pere.)

Hornung and McGee were the only ones I knew [that would sneak out after curfew]. I was too scared to even think about it. They didn't do it all the time—maybe on a Friday night. They were too tired to do it all the time. [Lombardi] would slack off toward the weekend. But during the week, nobody went anywhere.

BOB SKORONSKI

A fifth-round draft pick in 1956, Skoronski was an anchor at left tackle for most of his 11-year career with the Packers, although he shared the job with Norm Masters for most of Lombardi's first six years. Skoronski played as a rookie, went into the service for two years, returned for Lombardi's first season and played through 1968. He was the Packers' offensive captain when they won three straight NFL titles from 1965 to 1967 and was inducted into the Packers Hall of Fame in 1976.

I think [St. Norbert] fit the situation very well at the time. [De Pere] was a quiet little town where one could hardly get in trouble. A lot of the facilities were good. It was good to have the priests around. The food was excellent. I think the location and the peacefulness and the quietness of it was good for what our coach required at that time.

I think [Lombardi] liked it there. He liked Fr. Burke and all the people that he worked with there. One could always question whether he would have rather been in New York on the Hudson [River] training somewhere near where a lot of his friends and family were. But I truly believe he was very satisfied with it. He always was happy to get back there. He had everything he needed to operate. Never once did I hear him voice any dissatisfaction in anyway.

[Lombardi and Burke] had a great friendship. They were at ease talking to each other. They were informal. It was a good, close friendship more than a relationship. As you know, Coach Lombardi was a very good Catholic and that all fit together very well.

At the level I was at, I was like the janitor in the building, but [Burke] was a good guy. He was always upbeat about things, upbeat about what we were doing. Extremely, extremely friendly with everybody. I felt he enjoyed the guys being around. They were very respectful of him. They liked him a lot, kidded with him. That was a good arrangement.

He talked to a lot of players. He frequently was with Vince before supper. He came up and ate with us. As a result, he chatted with guys —as Vince did—when they came up from downstairs. He'd be talking about the day, how things were, joking, what have you in anticipation of the rookies singing their songs and that kind of stuff. He seemed to revel in that kind of stuff, along with Coach Lombardi.

I went to Mass sometimes. I was not a daily guy. Coach Lombardi was. Maybe one or two other guys were daily guys. We were very respectful of religion. We had a lot of guys who weren't Catholic who were involved in the Fellowship of Christian Athletes. There was a good strong feeling about the respect for religion and that was propagated by St. Norbert. You didn't have to be Catholic to be friends with Fr. Burke.

[Lombardi] was always in thought. That's the way he operated. He was an all-business kind of guy and if there was any levity, he brought it in and took it out. That's the way it was with him. Of course, we all sensed that. We knew from the beginning what he said was how it was going to be and there wasn't going to be any monkey business about it.

The greatest memory I have of St. Norbert was there was a soft ice cream store downtown. I can't remember the name of it; maybe a root beer stand. I remember one time, maybe after dinner, going down to the ice cream stand, getting a soft ice cream and walking back to the dormitory licking it. And as I got to the dormitory out walks Vince Lombardi with a couple coaches. I've got this cone in my hand and I put it behind my back so they don't see it. They walk by and everybody said, "Hello." Nothing happened. But I got to thinking, "Here I am, 32, 33 years old, and I'm hiding an ice cream cone from my coach. What's going on here? Maybe my time is up." It was later on [in my career]. [Lombardi] thought you got enough to eat where you were and it was the right stuff. I was with somebody else and don't remember who it was. [Lombardi] never said a word, never saw the cone, either. But I had some ice cream on the back of my pants.

After the [afternoon] session was over, Coach Lombardi and the coaches had their 5 o'clock club as I understand it. We had a little bit of our own 5 o'clock club [at Century Lanes]. We'd go over there, have a glass of beer and talk about the day's practice, have a few laughs and everybody would relax. Then we went back and had a dinner.

We had times when there were 15 or 20 [of us]. Not every day. But those hot days when you were prone to losing five or 10 pounds on the field in the afternoon, it was good to drink down a beer. We all enjoyed it. Nobody over-drank. It was a glass or two. It was a calmer. I thought it was good. I wouldn't promote it as something that has to happen in training camp, but we got it from the older guys and we carried it on and I'm sure they did it when we were gone.

A couple guys who had cars, we'd pile in and go over there. I doubt if anybody walked. You're not talking being there hours. You might be there 15, 20 minutes. You had to be to meals on time. After the meal was over, you had 45 minutes and had to be back in a meeting downstairs. So you had to be on your toes. There was no time for sleeping at that time of day.

A guy and his wife ran a place: Art Beecher. I never went there. I always went to Century Lanes. Dave [Hanner] was very good friends with him. One night during the season we'd take our wives out there for dinner, too. Dave was captain of the beer drinking club. He enjoyed his beer. I doubt if he went himself, but he might have because his friendship with Art was very good.

(Beecher owned Club Nicolet at 107 N. Sixth St., now Fort Howard Avenue.)

When we got in team meetings, [Lombardi] was very matter of

fact and kept moving on. He was very good at that. He had the teacher in him. When we first got in the major meeting, he'd talk about general stuff. Then we'd break off into groups. The offensive line would go one place and we'd cover stuff ourselves and get tested on plays and review what we were going to put in and look at some film. Then we'd get back together as an offense. Vince would put the group together again. It was extremely organized. It was timed. There was no bull. Nothing happened by accident in camp ever.

We were so close and there wasn't a lot of spread there, whether it was the mess hall or the meeting rooms or the dormitory rooms. But Lombardi time always works. It still works for me today and I'm 75. I still kind of operate on it and guys who were there talk about it to this day. That was one of the factors, in a small sense, to our success because it was discipline. You just can't get there on time and do it, you have to get there early. [Lombardi time] was at least 15 minutes early. If you were 10 minutes early, I guarantee you were looking behind you to see if [Lombardi] was there and thinking you could get a fine. And fines back then were costly because nobody made any money to speak of. You can understand why he did it. We were a group of guys very lax in what and how to do things, and he came in and started with the time. "Don't you guys come lollygagging in here at five minutes to nine for a nine o'clock meeting. You get here at 10 or 15 to and be sitting down looking at your book and be prepared to go. I don't want to lose time waiting for you to catch up."

PAUL HORNUNG

After winning the Heisman Trophy in 1956, Hornung was selected with the bonus, or first, pick of the 1957 draft. A quarterback at Notre Dame, he played there, and also at halfback and fullback during his first two years with the Packers. At that point, he appeared to be a player without a position and was contemplating early retirement. Lombardi put Hornung at halfback and turned him into a triple threat: a runner, a master of the option pass and a place-kicker. In Hornung's second season under Lombardi, he set an NFL scoring record with 176 points.

A year later, Hornung was named the league's Most Valuable Player.
He played from 1957 to 1966, other than the '63 season, when he was
suspended for gambling, and was inducted into the Pro Football Hall of
Fame in 1986.

We spent our life at St. Norbert. Absolutely! I'm coming out with
a new book. It's my last book. It's going to be called: "Run 'til
Daylight." Max and I were the most infamous members of the night
owl team. We had a wonderful time. We enjoyed it at St. Norbert. I
had a big argument with [Lombardi] one time. I told him, "We need
a night out. You let the married guys go home and get laid." He didn't
like that. I was mad as hell. I said, "The married guys get to go home
once a week. Shit, I'm 29 years old. I need a night out."

[Lombardi] was taking [bed] check. What happened was he forgot
his anniversary. He was out there looking at film every night and he
forgot. His wife called him up and said, "Happy anniversary, you son
of a bitch." So he didn't have anything to do and he wasn't going home.
So he decided to take check. He never took check. We could hear him
coming. I said [to McGee] pull that bed together. He looked in there
and here Max and I were in those two little beds in the middle of the
room. I had my arm around [McGee] and he had his arm around me.
I said, "Excuse us, Coach, you won't give us a night out, what the hell
are we going to do?" He didn't know whether to laugh or cry. He really
didn't. We caught him by surprise and he closed the door as if to say,
"What the hell is going on?" That was later. That was maybe my next
to last year.

Max snuck out every single night the year he was engaged. He
married this girl. It didn't last too long. It was Doug Sanders' ex-wife.
The golfer. [McGee] didn't miss one night in training camp. This was
later on after we had semi-retired from going out. So they didn't check
on us. I was 29, 30 years old by that time and wasn't going out with
anybody in town, but Max went out every night and he'd sneak back
in about 4 [a.m.].

[Lombardi] was very strict when it came to his rules. If you broke
them you had to pay the fiddler. [I got fined] three or four times [over

the years]. No more than that. One time, [Lombardi] said, "One of our brilliant party guys got caught again. This time, it's going to cost him $1,000." Back then if you were making $25,000 that was a lot of money. A $1,000 fine was a lot. And [Lombardi] said, "Next time it will be $5,000. And if you find somebody worth $5,000, I'll go with you." That was one of the best lines he ever got off.

I'll guarantee if [Lombardi] told the truth, he would have said he would have loved to go with us. He loved to play gin. He loved to play cribbage with us. He was a good man. He liked Max and I. Now, if we were screw-ups on the field, he wouldn't have liked it a bit. If you could play and you performed for him, he took that into consideration. If you were a guy who made mistakes on Sunday, you would have been fined three times more and maybe kicked off the team. Thank God, he never did that [with us].

I remember [after the first meeting], Bart said, "Things are going to be different around here." I had talked to [Lombardi] on the phone before. I was happy about what I had heard. A couple years, he made me come back early. He wanted to make sure I was in shape and he didn't want to risk me doing it on my own. He liked to push me. That was fine. I didn't mind.

We went for a beer or two once in awhile. I never drank much beer. [McGee] didn't either.

We enjoyed it [at St. Norbert]. It got to be kind of like home. Max and I had the same room for four, five years. After one of the exhibition games, they let the husbands go home and we had to go back to St. Norbert. After a couple drinks, I said, "I'm not going back." [McGee] talked me into it. He said, "Let's go back and then sneak out." I said, "OK." [But] I was mad. I said, "I don't care if he fines me." But [McGee] talked me into going back and then we snuck out.

I was downtown at the Northland Hotel. Max calls me. It's about seven o'clock in the morning. He says, "Get your ass out of there and I'll meet you outside the hotel." I said, "What are you talking about?" He said, "Do you have a car?" I said, "No. She picked me up." He said, "Well, I went back to the dorm about six o'clock and there was a note, 'See Coach Lombardi immediately.'" [McGee] went in and

[Lombardi] said, "Where's Hornung?" McGee said, "I don't know." [Lombardi] said, "I want to talk to you and him together. You go find him." So [McGee] calls me and says, "We got caught." We went back to St. Norbert and knocked on the door and [Lombardi] was in a meeting. He chewed our ass out. And I kind of lost my temper, too. [Lombardi] said, "What do you want to be: a playboy or a football player?" I said, "I want to be a playboy." [Lombardi] said, "Get out of here. I don't want to talk to you and it's going to cost you $1,500." It was during training camp. I said, "No, I'm not paying $1,500." And I said to McGee, "Let's go. Let's get out of here." Max said, "What?" I said, "Let's drive to Chicago right now. Screw it." Max said, "You gotta be kidding me." I said, "Nope. Let's go." But he wouldn't go with me. So I didn't go.

We always had the girls when we went out. We always had a date. We never went out without having a date. Like, on Wednesday night, we didn't have a meeting. We had until 11 o'clock. So we'd always go out.

TOM BETTIS

The Packers' first-round draft pick in 1955, Bettis played with the Packers from then through 1961. A middle linebacker, he started ahead of Ray Nitschke in Lombardi's first season and for part of the second. After Nitschke had won the job outright, Bettis was traded to Pittsburgh during training camp in 1962. Bettis played one year with the Steelers and then was a reserve on the Chicago Bears' NFL championship team in 1963. After his playing days, he spent 30 years in the NFL as an assistant coach, plus seven games in 1977 as interim head coach of the Kansas City Chiefs.

Practice didn't go very well the first couple of days. Vince was very dissatisfied. After our evening meal, we'd go into the study hall, wherever it was. Like an auditorium. He came in carrying a football and remarked about how unhappy he was about practice. Everybody was wondering why he had a football. There was a table there and he picked the ball up and said, "Gentlemen, we're going to start right from scratch. This is a football." Everybody was sort of shaking their head and Max McGee raised his hand. Vince said, "Yes, Max, what do you want?" He said, "Coach can you go a little slower." It broke everybody up and Vince sort of laughed and said, "OK, go on to your meetings with the coaches." That was 1959.

We had rules with Scooter [McLean], too, but they weren't enforced. It was more of a loosey-goosey operation. It was just a whole different atmosphere [under Lombardi]. But Vince came in thinking he was going to put out more than half the players. Put them on waivers. He didn't realize the talent we had at the time. His eyes were opened up after we got into training camp. He didn't walk into a place where there wasn't some talent.

JIM TEMP

A native of La Crosse and a three-time letterman at the University of Wisconsin, Temp played defensive end for the Packers from 1957 to 1960. He was a member of the Packers' executive committee from 1993 to 2003 and remains a director emeritus.

I was there [at Lombardi's first meeting], big as life, kind of in the back row. His famous quote was, "There are trains, planes and buses leaving Green Bay every day, and you might be on one." Very first meeting in what was like a Quonset hut. It was the evening before our first practice. I had not met him personally. He didn't call and say, "Jim, I want to talk with you." I might have seen pictures of him in the paper when he arrived in Green Bay. But I never shook his hand or met him until I walked into that meeting. What it sounded like was that he was going to work our asses off. The year before, Billy Howton had told Scooter McLean how to run the practices. He told him, "You don't want to run out our legs." It was just a joke. [Lombardi] was very authoritarian. It didn't sound like he was begging or cajoling. He was telling us straight facts about what he expected. It was a completely different approach than it had been under Lisle Blackbourn or Scooter McLean. I'd guess Lombardi talked maybe 45 minutes. I don't even remember him introducing his coaching staff. He just gave us a speech, what he expected of us. That we were going to win. That was it. Here was a guy coming in, he was the boss and he was going to run the show.

It was like night and day, black and white [between 1958 and '59]. It was unbelievable. Practice was timed. Every drill was a certain length. You weren't late for meetings. Nobody groused about anything. You took it as a man.

You'd walk across campus, climb into that old building. We had all of our meetings there during training camp. It was a metal building, wooden floor. It was set up like a classroom. Most of our meetings were separate: offense and defense. [Lombardi would] come in the defensive meeting and maybe walk around, but Phil [Bengtson] ran all of that. So I didn't see Lombardi much in the meetings. Scooter had meetings with all of us and he'd fall asleep occasionally when the film was running. One time the film broke. It was on those big reels and it was rolling off at his feet. It was at St. Norbert. Dave Hanner went, "Shhhhh. Don't say anything until he wakes up." Poor Scooter. He wanted to be friends with everybody and he thought he could do that and win.

I grew up in a Catholic grade school, Catholic high school, so I'd go to Mass in the morning. That was when they had Mass at 5:30, 6, 6:30, 7. They had so darn many priests. So I'd go to Mass and I'd always meet [Lombardi] coming or going. Some days, he'd go, "Hi Jim, how you doing? Beautiful day isn't it?" The next day, he'd walk by me with his head down and not even acknowledge me. It was at Mass on campus at the old St. Joseph Church. But very few players [went].

There were all different Norbertines who said Mass. Fr. Burke was the one who was with us all the time. I had played in the state Catholic [high school] basketball tournament there three years in a row, so I got to know Fr. Burke. He'd sit and chat. He was the only one I remember of all the White Fathers who was close to the Packers and, effectively, me because of that.

(The St. Norbert College Invitational Tournament, essentially the state basketball tournament for Catholic high schools, was played in Van Dyke Gym from 1936 to 1956. After the Catholic schools organized their own

athletic association, the tournament was officially recognized as a state tournament and was played at Van Dyke for two more years. Temp played at La Crosse Aquinas and was an all-tournament selection in 1950 when his team won the state championship.)

[Fr. Burke] was a wonderful guy. He was personable. He was interested in you. He was just a great, great priest. He'd always be around somewhere, either sitting on the steps or walking around looking to talk to players.

I was not one of [Lombardi's] boys. Maybe half the squad was and maybe half the squad wasn't. Hornung, McGee, Forrest Gregg, Bob Skoronski, Willie Davis. He'd demand things of them, too. But you knew that he knew those were his boys, the guys who were going to be able to win games for you. He'd compliment them if they made a play in practice. If I did something, there wouldn't be a word.

They made the rookies sing. I remember when Elijah Pitts; a big, tall black guy, Jim Brewington; and another black guy—we didn't have many back then—and they sang, *My Echo, My Shadow & Me.* They brought the roof down. Lombardi laughed so hard.

I remember after practice we'd all stop at a tavern and they would have all the beer iced down for us. I never went to Century Lanes. Right where the Black & Tan was, right next door, there was a tavern [Beecher's Club Nicolet] this fellow ran and he'd have the beer on ice for us. It would be [Dave] Hanner, [Jerry] Helluin when he was there, [Norm] Masters on occasion. Jerry Kramer. The six, seven, eight, 10 guys that I ran with, that's where we went. It was after the second practice. They'd bus us back and forth, and drop us off there. We'd sit and drink three, four beers until it was time for dinner and then we'd walk over to campus. Nobody got drunk. What we were basically doing was putting the liquid back in our bodies that we had just lost during the two practices.

NORM MASTERS

Masters was acquired by the Packers in 1957 in one of the biggest trades in club history and played through 1964. He was acquired as part of the blockbuster deal that sent quarterback Tobin Rote to the Detroit

Lions. During the Lombardi years, Masters split time at left tackle with Skoronski and also started at right tackle at times when Gregg filled in at guard due to an injury.

When you came into camp prior to Lombardi, you could stay at the dorm for a couple of days until veterans were supposed to report. The new line coach, Bill Austin, came in and said, "Hey, you're in camp." I said, "Yeah, I was thinking about playing golf." He said, "Well, I don't think so. Coach Lombardi says you're in camp and you're expected to be out at the field." That was the beginning where it registered with you that Lombardi was different. Then when you go out there, you wanted to die because it was so tough.

I met Lombardi in a downstairs recreation room. He was down there playing pool with some guys. They were in between practices. There were players down there and he was trying to connect. He was very cordial, but there was a certain presence about Lombardi that he was a person with authority and knowledge. I'm not saying that I got that the minute I met him. The way he responded was very cordial, but he wasn't buddy-buddy. He just said, "Good to have you here," and blah, blah, blah. Then when we went out to practice, you got the message that if you didn't bust your ass and did the different drills, you weren't going to be here.

You have to remember the only shade we had were two goal posts. And, in those days, they didn't believe in drinking water.

Lombardi had been preparing himself his whole life in my opinion. He wanted with a passion to become a head coach, and when he became a head coach he didn't need to wonder about what he'd do. He already had a plan. And that plan was to make sure people were in shape and had discipline. So he was committed to pushing people very hard. But what was interesting, there was never any push-back. I never saw a guy react to him. I've seen other coaches, other situations where players would get upset and it would be blah, blah this. But not a guy ever said anything [to Lombardi]. Never once did I hear a player talk back to him.

The point with Lombardi was that he got your respect because of how bright he was. And he loved when he was at St. Norbert when somebody left something on the board—a chemistry formula or whatever—to go up there and start monkeying with it to show he had knowledge beyond the football field. Apparently, he had taught some of those classes. He had been a teacher in high school, as well as a coach.

I use this as part of a joke: After the first meeting, I knew Lombardi really liked me. They say, "What do you mean?" He came to that meeting and talked about what he demanded, what he expected and so on. And he said, "Gentlemen, there are trains, planes and buses leaving here every day if you don't fit into this." And I've said, "At that moment, I knew he liked me." Why was that? I say, "Because I was the only guy who came by boat." I came from Michigan across the lake. I lived in Detroit and I took the ferry at Ludington across to Manitowoc.

We would practice in 90-degree heat, full pads, the whole nine yards. Guys would lose eight, 10 pounds of fluid. And we had two buses that would go from practice back to St. Norbert. We'd do wind sprints and you were dog tired. Of course, the bicycles were out there with the kids. All of a sudden you'd see these guys and everybody was rushing. They're rushing to get on the first bus. You wonder, "What the hell is the thing with the first bus?" You'd drink water when you got up to the locker rooms, but that first bus would go through De Pere and the majority of guys got off and went in and got a beer. They wanted to refurbish their liquids. The bus would pull in [to St. Norbert] sometimes with nobody on it. This was an outlet for guys to relax. Along that strip in De Pere, every other place was a tavern. Guys were drinking beer to replenish fluids. Then they'd try to avoid Lombardi when they got to the dining room. But Lombardi knew it probably—understood.

Then there was stuff on the bus. I remember Max McGee was sitting behind Jimmy Taylor, who was driving the bus, with rookies on it. And [McGee] had his hands over Jimmy's eyes: "A little left, a little right." We're going down the highway.

When you got to campus, you went straight to your rooms and lay down and tried to rest and drink water. Then you'd head over to the meetings. Then you'd go to bed. Lights out.

JERRY KRAMER

Kramer played for the Packers from 1958 to 1968 and was named the only offensive guard on the NFL's 50th anniversary team, which was selected in 1969. He has been a finalist in the voting for the Pro Football Hall of Fame 10 times or more than any player who hasn't been selected. He was inducted into the Packers Hall of Fame in 1975.

One of my clearest memories was when Joe Francis and I came back to Green Bay. Jack Vainisi was the [business] manager and the veterans reported three days later than the rookies. Joe was from Oregon and I was from Idaho, so Joe rode back with me. We got to Green Bay and didn't have a place to stay. We were at the Packer office downtown and we were talking to Vainisi. "Jack, you gotta get us a place to stay." "Well, the dorms aren't open." I said, "Jack, we need a place to stay. Motels are eight bucks, man. That's pretty expensive." So we're trying to get him to open the dorm and Coach Lombardi walked by. That was the first time I had ever seen him. And he didn't stop to say, "Hey, how you doin? What's up? How is it going? I'm the coach." It was *(at that point, Kramer proceeded to say in a gruff, snarly voice)*: "What's the matter?" "These guys need a place to stay and the dorm isn't open yet." "Get it open and put them in a dorm." Then he turned around and was gone. They opened the dorm, and Joe and I moved in, went out that night and had a few beers, and were kind of relaxing. The next day, we're heading down the steps and Coach Lombardi was at the bottom: "Where the hell you think you're going?" "We're going to go play golf." I had a golf bag over my shoulder. He said, "The hell you are. You're in the dormitory. You make all meals, all meetings, all practices just like everybody else. Go get dressed." So we put our golf clubs back and go to practice twice a day for the next couple days. And they were killers. He was just absolutely trying to impress upon us the seriousness of it and what he was doing, the whole thing. It was from the golf course to Dachau in one fell swoop. That was my first introduction to him.

(During Lombardi's first four seasons the Packers' office building was located at 349 S. Washington St. in downtown Green Bay.)

I remember the first meeting, I think, and there's a little divergence on that. He said, "If you're not willing to be part of a team—to subjugate your individual needs, wishes, wants and egos for the benefit of the team—then get the hell out." He hesitated and stopped and said something like, "There are planes and trains and buses every day leaving here and some of you may be on them." We looked at one another and said, "This guy can't be that serious. It'll be tough. But that was a little over the top." We had no idea what was in store and what he meant. But we sure as hell found out pretty quick.

I remember Bill Austin repeating over and over and over: "The one-man, the one-man. Then you block the two-man. You pull." Then all of sudden, Coach Austin wasn't looking at us anymore. We're wondering what the hell's going on? We turn around and there's Coach Lombardi in the back of the room. So Austin is telling us what to do, but you could see he was a little uncomfortable in his role as a coach. That sweep, to me, kind of evolved. They put in the basic blocking, but I don't remember a blackboard talk that [Lombardi] had where he talked about execution and how the sweep could go here or here or here. I've seen it on television a lot, but I don't remember it from camp.

I remember [Lombardi] coming down the hallway one night. My room was right across from Hornung and McGee's and down one. [Bill] Quinlan was in door two with Dan Currie. A couple other guys here, there. So we used to congregate in my room a little bit. I had the cribbage board, music and what not. We ordered pizza in one night; it was 11 o'clock curfew and it must have been quarter to 12 or something like that. We must have gotten by the early bed check and everybody is in my room, and they're all bare-naked. St. Norbert didn't have air conditioning, so we were all in our birthday suits and eating pizza. I'm standing by the door and I have a premonition and lean out the door and look down the hallway. I look into Coach Lombardi's face about 10, 15 feet away. I don't say anything and lean back in. There's no point in warning anybody; just wait for the storm to hit. He came in and started chewing ass. He fined us all 50 bucks. "I don't know what the hell you're thinking about?" Blah, blah, blah. Then he

[left] and he was staying across the lawn in a different area. Pat Peppler was staying up there too and then he comes into the room. He's laughing and giggling. Lombardi must have told him, "You should have seen them. They're all bare-ass naked, eating pizza." Lombardi chewed us unmercifully and he made us run extra laps the next day. But he must have been laughing his ass off when he was telling Peppler [about us]. They both must have thought it was funny.

I don't remember Bart Starr very well [that first year]. Bart was like methane gas: colorless, odorless, tasteless, virtually invisible. He couldn't create a controversy if he wanted to. Joe Francis was there and vying for the job. Lamar McHan was half a psycho case. He'd get all pissed up and get on Coach Lombardi and make a fool of himself. And Vito, Vito, Vito. Babe [Parilli] was a capable guy, a competent guy. He was part of that mix.

I remember when Howie Ferguson got cut and that had a big impact on me. Fergie was a rompin', stompin', tough S.O.B. He gave you every-thing he had, every opportunity. He was running with a shoulder that should have been wired together. He just had a lot of heart. So I was surprised when he got traded. I got a look at the downside of the game for a guy literally giving it everything he had and he had done it for some time. But the young boy [Jimmy Taylor] comes along and takes his spot. That was a sad thing for me. Howie was Hornung's bud. He was one of the studs, one of the guys we didn't think would be let go. So it did send a message: Your job is only as good as your last game. Every year there will be a bunch of new boys coming in here and look-ing for your job.

Royce Whittington. Big boy from Louisiana. He had been drafted about 270 and weighed about 315. He put on a lot of weight because he thought he was going to be an NFL player and they were all big. But he forgot about being able to move. I remember a kid named Luis Hernandez. Luis was overweight. He was the last guy around the post on our laps, the last guy over to our area to do our drills. He was the last guy up to the sled and he was slow hitting the sled. Coach Lombardi told him several times to speed it up. About the third day, we're running the sweep and Hernandez is slow. Coach Lombardi screams,

"Hernandez, you're not only fat and slow, you're stupid." That was the end of Luis Hernandez. He was gone the next day.

We played cribbage every year in St. Norbert as long as I could remember. I would always have the cribbage board and we'd have a little tournament. It seems like guys would throw in five bucks. Max and I were hard-core players. We loved to play poker, too. But you couldn't get a poker game together that quick.

Willie [Davis] and I were pretty good friends along the way. I found out a little bit about his background, his M.B.A., his intelligence and his thoughtfulness. And we started talking about business opportunities. So we went to a new steakhouse—can't remember the name of it now—that was a franchise place and had opened in Green Bay. We looked at it and were coming back and talking about franchises and life after football. Skoronski was selling rings for Josten's and almost all of the guys had jobs one way or the other. Don Chandler, who had been my roommate the year before, decided not to come back. I'm not exactly sure how it happened, but maybe Willie said, "I see you lost your roommate." And I said, "Yeah, why don't you come be my roommate?" It was a natural thing between two veterans who were looking toward the end of their careers. I don't think we thought much about color or that we were different color. I remember talking to Willie one of the first nights we were together. Lights out and I couldn't get to sleep. I said, "Hey, Will, do you believe in white power?" This was the time of Malcolm X and the [Black Panthers] and the unrest in society and the riots. He says, "No, J. I don't believe in white power." "Hey, Will, you believe in black power?" He says, "No, J. I don't believe in black power." "Hey, Will, what the hell you believe in?" "Green power, J." No [it had nothing to do with breaking new ground]. We still don't know today if we were the first mixed roommates. We've never found it important to look it up or be concerned about it.

JESSE WHITTENTON

Whittenton started at right cornerback for the Packers during Lombardi's first six seasons as coach. He signed with the Packers as a free agent before the 1958 season after spending his first two years with the Los Angeles Rams. Whittenton's last season with the Packers was 1964.

We showed up the day before the reporting date. We went out on the town, partying and all that stuff. The first thing Vince came out with was: McGee, Hornung, Whittenton, Ferguson, it's going to cost each of you 250 bucks. Howie says, "For what?" [Lombardi] said, "Because you missed curfew last night." [Howie] said, "Training camp doesn't start until today." [Lombardi] said, "Mister, it started when you put your luggage in that dormitory." He told us that in a meeting. Practice didn't start until the next day. I paid the $250. No, [I didn't say anything]. Neither did Hornung nor McGee. Ferguson was the only one who said anything.

That was just one big party [in 1958]. Scooter played poker with us. We just had a ball. He'd play poker with us on the plane.

Oh yeah [players broke curfew under Lombardi]. I got caught. Fuzzy Thurston, Lew Carpenter and I think Boyd Dowler. We were out at a nightclub dancing and all that stuff. We came back in for curfew and went back out. Everybody involved went back out. I think Jerry Kramer was involved also. I was standing up at the bar and happened to look at the front door, and Red Cochran walked in. I ducked behind the bar. When he left, the phone rang and the bartender said, "It's for you." He handed it to me and Red said, "You guys get your asses back over to that dormitory and get in bed because I'm going to pull a bed check now." So I told the guys, "We've got to go because Red is going to pull bed check." They said, "Ah, Red won't turn us in." I was the only one who came back.

They all got fined. And [Lombardi] made us stay after practice and do leapfrogs around the football field. All the spectators were laughing. It was just to embarrass us. [Lombardi] didn't say anything other than, "When practice is over, line up."

LEW CARPENTER

Carpenter was a jack-of-all trades for the Packers from 1959 to 1963. He played halfback and offensive end, filled in at fullback, was the designated emergency quarterback, and returned punts and kickoffs. Lombardi acquired Carpenter in the trade that sent Howton to Cleveland before the 1959 season. After he quit playing, Carpenter served as an assistant coach in the NFL for 31 years, including a year in Washington when Lombardi was head coach of the Redskins and later for 11 years with the Packers.

I remember driving into St. Norbert, trying to find a place to park, trying to find the dorm and all that. I had gone to the office downtown and signed my contract. I came up earlier and that's when I first met Lombardi. I remember the first thing he said in our meetings: "Just remember one thing: if you're 10 minutes early, you might be 10 minutes late."

Max McGee was my roommate in training camp. I roomed with McGee every year and I was there five years. He was always my roommate in training camp. Hornung was a good boy compared to Max. Hornung got accused of a lot of things, but Max was the culprit. Most of the time I was asleep before the bed-check guy came in at 11 o'clock. Then maybe 30 minutes later, Max would take off. He'd just go and come when he wanted to. I think he'd just put his clothes on and leave. They'd have double-checks some times and I guess he got caught. But that's the way Max was. He was really the fair-haired boy of Vince's. If Max would drop a football in practice, Vince would chew him out. But you know Max's personality. He'd say, "Coach, some you catch, some you drop." Vince would just laugh. McGee was the only one who could get by with that stuff. Lombardi knew how to deal with people. I guess he thought if he got tough on Max like he did with Hornung and Taylor, he'd go the other way.

Max would get back to the room in time for a wake-up call and to eat breakfast. He didn't do it every night. Maybe once or twice a week. He'd stay out past 12 or 1 o'clock. Many times, I'd get up to go to the bathroom and he wouldn't be there.

He never brought anybody back when I was there. Oh gosh, I don't know what Vince would have done if he would have found some woman in the dorm.

I went to a little bar near St. Norbert, not too far from campus. Buck's—that was the name of it. Jesse Whittenton went to Century Lanes and one night I went with him. It was about five minutes to 11 and I said, "Jesse, we've got to get our asses back to St. Norbert." He said, "OK." So we jump in the car and we're speeding. All of a sudden we get close to St. Norbert and a state patrolman's lights start blinking as we drive into the parking lot. We get out of the car and the patrolman says, "Not you, again, Jesse." He had gotten him many times.

The dorm rooms were small and had two beds. They were only about twice as wide as your butt. You could hardly roll over without rolling off the bed. But it was all right. Most of the time in training camp, you were so damn tired you'd go right to sleep.

The camps with Lombardi were the most highly conditioned of the different teams I played with. I think his belief was that anybody can react under normal circumstances. But in football, you needed to react when you're tired. We used to do ups-and-downs and hit the sled before we ever started practice. Before you even started calisthenics, you had all these drills you had to go through.

BOYD DOWLER

Dowler was voted the NFL's Rookie of the Year by United Press International in Lombardi's first season. Although he had played quarterback at Colorado, Dowler was chosen by the Packers in the third round of the 1959 draft as a receiver. Dowler was actually selected prior to Lombardi being named coach, but that was the position he played for 11 years with the Packers. Dowler was inducted into the Packers Hall of Fame in 1978. After he was done playing, he served as an assistant coach and NFL scout for 25 years.

Looking west, a view of Main Avenue in West De Pere. The street was a center of activity when the Lombardi Packers trained at St. Norbert, starting in 1959. (De Pere Historical Society)

Derrick's A&W Root Beer Stand at 420 Main Avenue in West De Pere was a popular place for the Lombardi Packers to go for treats. (De Pere Historical Society)

The Prom Ballroom, located just west of U.S. Highway 41 and just south of Main Avenue in West De Pere, was a popular hangout for 18- to 21-year olds during the 1960s when they could legally drink in Wisconsin's beer bars. Marv Fleming went there as a rookie and was chided for it when Vince Lombardi found out. (De Pere Historical Society)

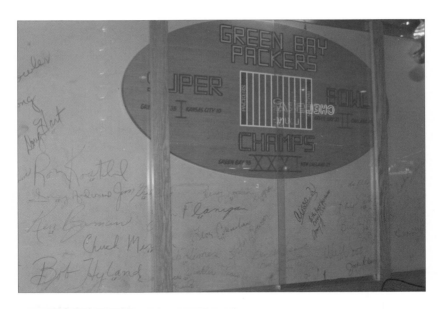

Autographs of many of the
Lombardi Packers can still be seen
today at Century Lanes in De Pere.
The players started signing on the
wall in 1968, the year Lombardi
served as general manager.

Fr. Rowland C. De Peaux

Players walk from Sensenbrenner Hall on the sidewalk along Second Street, when it still cut through campus. (Green Bay Press-Gazette archives)

Herb Adderley (right) befriended Jim Hughes, who as a young boy hung out on campus almost daily during training camp. Hughes grew up on Marsh Street, virtually across the street from Sensenbrenner Hall.

Lombardi and personnel director Pat Peppler sit on the steps of Sensenbrenner Hall waiting for the players to report in 1964. Clips of Lombardi greeting the players on the doorstep of the dorm that year were filmed for the documentary, Run to Daylight. (Green Bay Press-Gazette archives)

Fr. Brendan McKeough

From left, John C. Cosline, president of Milwaukee Chapter, St. Norbert College Alumni Association, Fr. Dennis Burke and Lombardi pose with award at the Milwaukee alumni meeting. (Green Bay Press-Gazette archives)

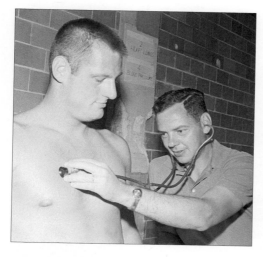

Second-year defensive end Ben Davidson is examined by Dr. Joseph Grace at the start of camp in 1962 when physical exams were given on the St. Norbert campus. Davidson was traded that summer to Washington and later played against the Packers in Super Bowl II as a member of the Oakland Raiders. (Green Bay Press-Gazette archives)

Veteran defensive end Bill Quinlan has his ears checked by Dr. E.R. Killeen during physical exams in 1959. (Green Bay Press-Gazette archives)

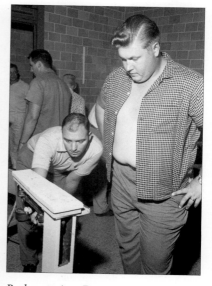

Packers trainer Domenic Gentile adjusts the scale as he weighs rookie lineman Royce Whittington during physical exams at St. Norbert on the eve of the first practice in 1961. Whittington reported overweight at 319 pounds and was cut by Lombardi the next morning while he was running a lap around the practice field. (Green Bay Press-Gazette archives)

From left, Packers' assistant coaches Tom Fears, Red Cochran, Bill Austin, Norb Hecker and Phil Bengtson stand with the head coach on the St. Norbert campus in 1959, Lombardi's first season with the Packers.(Green Bay Press-Gazette archives)

The Packers watch film in a classroom on the St. Norbert campus in 1961. Lombardi is standing in background. (Green Bay Press-Gazette archives)

From left, veterans Boyd Dowler, Paul Hornung and Ray Nitschke are greeted by Lombardi as they sit in the cafeteria at the Sensenbrenner Memorial Union in late July, 1962. (Green Bay Press-Gazette archives)

Packer players eating a meal in the cafeteria at St. Norbert. From left to right: defensive end Jim Temp, offensive tackle Norm Masters, quarterback Lamar McHan, quarterback Joe Francis and fullback Jim Taylor (standing).

Lombardi shakes the hand of rookie tackle Jack Petersen as players arrive at Sensenbrenner Hall in 1964. Petersen, an 11th-round draft pick from Nebraska-Omaha, didn't make the team, but the scene was captured by a cameraman filming Run to Daylight.

Defensive end Jim Temp stands in the cafeteria line.

Packers' quarterbacks (from left, John Roach, Bart Starr, Val Keckin and Joe Francis) pose on the St. Norbert campus in August, 1961. Neither Keckin nor Francis made the team that year. (Green Bay Press-Gazette archives)

I was playing in the College All-Star Game so I didn't get up there until after the first preseason game. We played the Bears in Milwaukee on a Saturday night and the College All-Star Game was the night before in Chicago. I caught a train from Chicago to Milwaukee and dressed out for the Bear game. Then we went back to Green Bay and we started back in practice Monday and I was out there.

(The College All-Star Game was a showcase exhibition played from 1934 to 1976 between the defending NFL champion and a team of the best college seniors from the previous season. When it started it was viewed by some as even bigger than the NFL championship. It became less significant as the years passed and was finally canceled. But as long as it was played, a team's best rookies usually would report to training camp late.)

As far as remembering the campus and stuff, it didn't impact me much right away. I thought it was a nice enough place, but I was primarily thinking about what was going on on the field.

I remember my room number: 123. That was after the first year. The first year it was on a different side. It was toward the front of the building. After that, it was around on the side. I roomed there with Ron Kramer until he [left]. Then I roomed with Fuzzy until he retired. Then I roomed with Lee Roy Caffey. Then I left. My final 10 years, I stayed in the same room. Ron and I didn't request rooming with another, we just came back that second year with Vince and they put us together. Billy Butler was my roommate the first year. He was a running back from Chattanooga. We were both rookies. I was fortunate. The guys I roomed with I also was good friends with.

We didn't waste any energy doing anything, but practicing football. If anybody ever did, I didn't know about it. If they had a swimming pool [at St. Norbert], I didn't know about it. If they had a tennis court, I didn't know about it. If they had a gym, I didn't know where it was. I just ate, slept and had meetings out there. That went on for 11 years with me.

The big building where the chow hall, the dining room, was wasn't built yet. It's like a student union building and that's where we ate our meals after that. But the first year, we ate in a different, older building. I'm not sure if it was another dorm. It was just beyond Sensenbrenner, down more into the interior of the campus.

We had meetings across the square, or mall, sometimes in the earlier years. When we all got together sometimes we'd meet there because it was a little bigger. That may have been the first couple years. After that, I think all our meetings were downstairs in Sensenbrenner.

I never remember [Lombardi] not being in a meeting. Everybody on the team would be in a meeting and he may have had a few words to say or a lot of words to say. Then the defense would split and go to another meeting room. [Lombardi] was basically the offensive coordinator, although nobody used that term in those years. After he talked about what he needed to talk about in the meeting with all of the offense, we'd break down and the offensive line would leave. All the backs and receivers, along with the quarterbacks, would stay and go over the pass offense, while the offensive line coach would take the line. [Lombardi would stay] with the backs and ends. I was involved with him in the meetings almost all the time.

He was a tremendous teacher. Very direct. Very thorough. He was a very good communicator. Very strong delivery. His voice, as everyone knows, was unusual. He had a presence about him. Let's say, you made sure you paid attention. He wasn't dull. He was interesting to listen to. He knew what he was talking about. He'd be up there with a piece of chalk at the board and sometimes he'd emphasize a point and break the chalk off. Let's say he was intense. He didn't repeat himself a lot. He was well organized. [The meetings] weren't overdone. But he went through every position. He didn't leave anything to chance. He didn't nitpick or talk on and on and on. And he wasn't in there trying to trip you up. He wasn't asking questions to see if you were paying attention. He knew on the practice field if you were paying attention.

When he'd get upset was when we were watching films of the prior game. If it was in the preseason, it would be on Sunday evening at 7:30 when we had to report after a Saturday night game. We got most of [Sunday] off. We had to be there at dinner at 6 o'clock. The first thing he did with the whole team was talk about the game. Somewhere in there, he was liable to get a little upset, depending on how we played. But he didn't neglect to tell us when things were good, either. He was equal in his praise. But he was very direct about that, too. He didn't mince any words. Basically, the other coaches didn't say much. When he put the offensive film on the projector and started going, he broke down every play very thoroughly and you didn't get away with anything. If you missed a block or screwed up or did anything at all, he didn't just let it go. He was into you and sometimes he'd get into you pretty hard. That's just the way he was. And he was just as hard on Hornung and Taylor and Forrest Gregg—although he didn't have to get on Forrest much—as anyone else. He didn't pick out some rookie, some guy who wasn't going to be out there on Sunday and make a scapegoat out of him. He'd jump on anybody. No one was immune from criticism.

I remember the worst he ever got was when we spent a week in Pewaukee my rookie year. He usually took us away for a week anyway. He was absolutely ballistic watching the film. That was his first year. Something set him off.

The thing that got him the worst were mental mistakes. That got him worse than if you dropped a ball or missed a block—that sort of thing, he might say, "You gotta do better than that now," or something like that. What he really got upset about were [things like] jumping offside, lack of concentration.

[Lombardi] ate every meal with us. He went to every meeting with us. We weren't out about the campus very much. We'd walk across the square, you'd see him. He had a room out there, although I'm not sure he stayed many nights at all. But he was around. The 7:30 [p.m.] meeting would last until 9, at least, then we had an 11 o'clock curfew. There wasn't a whole lot of down time.

You weren't supposed to drive your car to practice from St. Norbert. You were supposed to take the bus. Now, you could get around that every now and then after you'd been there a few years. After we bought our home in Green Bay, I used to take my car and park in the parking lot [outside the Packers offices] in the morning. I lived only six, seven minutes from the stadium and I'd drive home to have lunch with my wife. They used to count plates to see if you were at lunch. [Lombardi] would get a little lax, but he made a mention to me one time, "You better start coming to lunch." He knew how many people were there, but you could get away with it once in awhile.

I was in a wing [at Sensenbrenner] where a lot of the black guys were right down the hall or across the hall. Willie Wood. Willie Davis. [Herb] Adderley. [Bob] Jeter. They'd usually group up and I'd go over and sit there and laugh while they told stories. Nitschke and Carroll Dale lived just one room down from us on the same wing. You'd go over and sit in somebody's room and shoot the bull, yeah. But a lot of times, like after lunch, you'd go lie down and fall asleep for a little while. You had a couple hours. After lunch you didn't have meetings in the afternoon during two-a-days. After two-a-days were over, we'd have a 3 o'clock or 3:30 meeting. The only meetings we had during two-a-days were at night. Once we started practicing once a day, we would meet twice a day: one at night and once in the afternoon. Wednesday night we had off. We didn't have to go meetings. We had to go to dinner, but like married guys could go home until 11.

[Players going out and having a wild time on Wednesday nights] was known to happen from time to time. You had from 6:30 until 11. You can have a lot of fun in four hours. It wasn't everybody. I don't think Bart and Carroll ever went out. Of course, you had Hornung and McGee. Jerry and Fuzzy. Ron Kramer. Myself. Herb and Willie were out. They'd go to Speed's. Some guys would go out to eat: have a few pops and a dinner and bounce around town a little. On some occasions, some [players] might have had a little more than they should.

(Speed's Cocktail Lounge, located at 327 N. Monroe Ave. on Green Bay's near east side, was a favorite hangout of the Packers in the late Fifties and early Sixties.)

CHAPTER 5

The Players (Part 2)

WILLIE DAVIS

Davis was acquired in a trade with the Cleveland Browns for end A.D. Williams just 10 days before the start of training camp in 1960. Whereas Williams, who was in his second year, played just one season with the Browns and caught just one pass, Davis enjoyed a Hall of Fame career. Davis played left defensive end for the Packers from 1960 to 1969 and was inducted into the Pro Football Hall of Fame in 1981.

The trade had been made in July. I was heading up [to Green Bay] for the first time. I remember going across the bridge and it was so quiet and serene.

I don't think I'll ever forget that day. I was driving along Highway 57 and I get in De Pere. I get across the bridge and go to St. Norbert and I was met by Jack Vainisi. He said, "Let me take you to the coach." Boy, that was a moment that impacted the rest of my life. [Lombardi] could be one of the most cordial and warmest individuals when he wanted to be. He said, "Hey, Willie." And he wanted to know right away if I remembered him from the Giants. I said, "Yeah." He said, "Well, let me tell you something. One of the interests I had in you came from seeing you make a play against the Giants. I don't think I ever saw an individual display more quickness and reaction than you showed on that play." He said, "Just so you know, we think you can come here and play for us."

He said, "Willie, I know Cleveland played you at both offense and defense." He said, "I'm telling you in advance, we're interested in you coming here and concentrating on defensive end for us." He told me that beforehand and at St. Norbert. See, when I got traded to Green Bay, I was in Cleveland and had spent the day as a substitute teacher on the west side of [the city]. I was driving home and heard about the trade in my car. When I got home, Jack [Vainisi] had called. But I had signed a contract two weeks before that with Cleveland and was told by Eddie Ulinksi, who was my position coach, and Coach [Paul] Brown that I was going to be the starting left tackle. That I had graded second best on the team. When I'm driving home and there's a sports flash, "Willie Davis, second-year offensive tackle, traded to the Green Bay Packers," I was crushed. I just didn't know what to think. I don't think I ever had anything hit me with more surprise as related to football.

That was the year [the league] had expanded to Dallas. And Dallas took Nate Borden, who had been [the Packers'] left end. And [the Packers] had Jim Temp and he had some shoulder surgery. So I think in the first scrimmage, I went in like the second play and I started every game the Packers played for the next 10 years.

We mainly just stayed in the dormitory [at St. Norbert]. There was no practice field. We just lived in the dormitory, ate at the student union and that was kind of it. I remember the first meetings we had every year. [Lombardi would] say, "Hey this is who we are, this is where you are and this is what we're going to do." He left no doubt that if you were going to hang around and be a part of it, you were going to have to do that. We always had that [first meeting] downstairs there and you had to leave that knowing he was very serious.

You know what was interesting? Forrest Gregg and I very seldom went after each other. It was kind of like if Lombardi was focused on the offense and he was looking at him and he was a little upset, I'd let Gregg block me without as much resistance. It was the other way if [Lombardi] was focused on the defense. Then Gregg would cut me some space. [Lombardi] kind of accepted that. With John Sutro, I probably wasn't focused on beating him and I guess he told Forrest, "Willie isn't that hard to block. I handled him OK." You know guys can't wait to tell you stuff like that. It was just Forrest saying, "Hey, man, this guy is saying he had no problems blocking you." I think it was over at dinner [at the Union]. I said, "Well, that's interesting." By then Sutro had become a little more mouthy than you were accustomed to from a typical rookie. The next day, I had a pretty good day. I had good motivation.

I think Paul [Hornung] and Max [McGee] were the only two guys who had the nerve [to sneak out after curfew]. If you were a new guy, you were probably scared to death. With me, I wasn't prepared to let Coach Lombardi catch me doing anything.

MARV FLEMING

Drafted in the 11th round in 1963, Fleming played seven years with the Packers and was the starting tight end on their three straight NFL championship teams from 1965 to 1967, including the first two Super Bowl winners. Fleming played out his option in 1969, signed with Miami and played in three more Super Bowls with the Dolphins. He was inducted into the Packers Hall of Fame in 2010.

My experience at St. Norbert was that the rooms were very small. The reason I say that is I was rooming with Lionel Aldridge and Lionel took most of the room. He would lay his coat on my side. I'd say one-fourth of his stuff was on my side. The day came where I drew a line with chalk down the middle of the room and said, "This is your side. And this is my side." Lionel didn't take that the right way. We had known each other since high school. He was from northern Cal and I was from southern Cal, and we played against each other in a high school Shrine game. Then he went to Utah State and I went to Utah. Then it exploded. If you could see two bears getting into it in a room, that's what we did. I was the boxer. If Lionel was here, he'd say, "Yeah, Marv won." When I came out of the room, everybody was outside in the hall. I opened the door and I think it was Red Cochran who said, "What happened to you?" I said, "I tripped and fell." Lionel came out all bloodied, too, and [Cochran] said, "I guess you tripped and fell, too." That was the last time we were roommates. We were still friends, but a guy has to have his space. That's what I remember about those rooms: They were so small. You had a bed, a little desk, your closet on one side and that was it. The beds were long enough, I think.

Dave [Robinson], myself and Lionel called [ourselves] "The Bookends." We sang the song, *On Broadway*, but we changed Broadway to Green Bay. It goes something like, "They say the [neon] lights are bright in Green Bay." And there's a part that says you won't make it. "They say I won't last too long in Green Bay … . But they're [dead] wrong I know they are 'cause I'm going to be a football star." It was a great song. Everybody loved it. They always wanted us to sing that song. I think we were the rookies that made the team. I was back-up. Rob was back-up, too. Lionel was the singer. We'd get applause and all that. "Sing, more, more, more." We sang that thing well. [Lombardi] was smiling. First of all, we had rhythm. And Lionel had a great voice; a great, great voice. We learned the words. We even made a record of it in Green Bay somewhere. Some person made it for us.

The thing for me as a rookie was that when I came there, I never drank alcohol. For rookie day, they took me out and got me drunk—one of the bars on Main Street. This was after we made the team. I was sick for a couple days and Lombardi was pissed.

I remember a rookie. Don't remember his name or anything, but he was from Wisconsin. Maybe he went to Madison. It was his whole life's dream to make the Green Bay Packers. His parents' dream, all his uncles' and aunts'. After lunch, we'd look at films. The kid fell asleep. When the lights came on, Lombardi stretches and turns around and sees the kid sleeping. Lombardi says—he whispers—"When the guy wakes up, tell him he's fired."

Most of the guys were married and they'd go home to their wives. They'd get back just before 11 o'clock.

When I was a rookie, I used to go to a place called The Prom. At roll call, one time: "Henry?" "Yo." "Willie?" "Yo." "Fleming?" "Yo."

[Then Lombardi says], "By the way Fleming, stay out of the teen joints." I said, "Coach, I'm not old enough to go to the big bars." He says, "Stay home then. The babysitters are coming home and saying they're seeing a Packer there." I couldn't go to Speed's and all those places the guys hung out. I wasn't old enough. I was a Packer player, but I wasn't old enough.

(The Prom Ballroom was located on the far west side of West De Pere on the property where the BP, A&W and Taco Bell complex is located today. It was a beer bar frequented by people under the age of 21 when 18 was the drinking age in Wisconsin.)

My experience in Green Bay and at St. Norbert was one of the better experiences anyone could have in their life. Being with a group of guys and a coach—I spoke to a group not long ago and said, "If any other team would have had Coach Lombardi, they would have won." Lombardi made me as a player. Although he was a taskmaster, you have to have taskmasters.

One time as a rookie, [Lombardi] said, "All right offense, I want you to watch [No.] 81. Watch him. This guy wants to play football." I hit the defensive end and knocked him down and then went over and tried to hit somebody else. I always tried to get two guys on a play. Then he says, "Turn the lights on." And he goes crazy. "Damn it! He wants to play! He wants to play! But if he learned his plays and blocked the right man each time, he'd be a better ballplayer. But he did something. He hit somebody." Three different plays, I blocked the wrong guy. But I blocked them and made the play go. And one time, I got up and was blocking somebody else.

You know what I remember? They had a root beer stand near the campus, a couple blocks away. I used to go there all the time. Root beer floats. In the evenings, I'd walk over to the root beer stand. I'd go by myself. I was a loner. I didn't drink, remember? I went to a Mormon school.

(There was an A&W Root Beer Stand located at 420 Main Ave. in West De Pere.)

DAVE ROBINSON

Robinson was drafted in the first round in 1963 and was a stalwart at left outside linebacker until he was traded to the Washington Redskins in 1973. He became a starter late in his rookie year and emerged as a dominant player as the Packers won three straight titles from 1965 to 1967. He was inducted into the Packers Hall of Fame in 1982.

First of all, I played in the All-Star Game. The team went back to Green Bay, but I had to fly home because my wife was pregnant. It was our first child and we were having twins. She was having a lot of trouble. So I flew home to New Jersey, left a car at the airport, and then flew back to O'Hare and then drove to Green Bay by myself. I pulled into St. Norbert College; I couldn't believe it. The school was so small and Sensenbrenner Hall was so small. I had been on a college campus at Penn State. That was a huge campus. I couldn't believe how small the campus was and how close the downtown was. And, then, my first real recollection was that god-awful smell from the paper mills. I thought: "What in the world is this?"

Then I was told by Pat Peppler that it says, "The meeting is at 1 o'clock, but if I were you, I would not be later than quarter of." So I got there at 12:30. I wasn't going to let Vince get mad at me. Plus, he told me he wanted me to come to camp at 245 or 240 [pounds]. I had never been over 225 in my life. I had beefed up and done everything else to try and get to 240. Just before I went for my first weigh-in, I drank a half-gallon of orange juice or sugar water juice. I weighed in at 239. That was at the stadium the next day. Monday morning. I went out to practice, came back in and I think I was 229 or 227. I couldn't hold onto it.

The first time I met Lombardi, I flew in—part of my signing bonus was that they arranged for me to buy a car dirt cheap at Brown County Motors—and picked the car up in late January, early February. I met Vince at the old offices down at the Downtowner Motel. That was another thing that shocked me. I go to the Downtowner Motel; this is where the Green Bay Packers' offices are?

I go, "This is really a fly-by-night operation. What did I get myself into?" When I came back after the All-Star Game, they were in the new offices at City Stadium, which is now Lambeau Field. And I felt a lot better.

This was my livelihood so I read everything I could about Lombardi and the Green Bay Packers and their ballplayers and everything else. I was out in the waiting room [at the old offices] and I heard him bellow in the back in that real heavy voice of his. I knew he was one of the "Seven Blocks of Granite." I knew he was a guard in college. And I knew guards were pretty big. So I expected a big guy to come walking out. When he walked out, my first impression was, "Damn, he's small to be a guard." But he left nothing to the imagination. He was the boss. He was the man. It was in his voice, in his demeanor, everything else. I was very impressed right away.

I was born in South Jersey and went to Penn State. I had been south of the Mason-Dixon Line only a couple of times and they weren't pleasurable trips. I looked at the team and saw that there were an awful lot of people from Texas, a quarterback from Alabama, a running back from Louisiana, another from Louisville. There were a lot of Southerners on the team and white Southerners. I was a little apprehensive. But, boy, that first meeting at St. Norbert College, I walked in and sat down, and [realized] there was no black or white. They were all Packers. Some of my best friends on the team became guys from the South. Guys like Bart Starr opened their arms to you. Paul Hornung is someone I'm still close to, although he wasn't there that year. I liked his laissez-faire, devil-may-care attitude. All the guys. Henry Jordan was from Virginia and he was just super right away.

You have to understand I was a first-round draft choice. Vince Lombardi had built a real strong unit. Everybody was like family. The first-round draft choice is a guy who you assume is going to make the team. That means one of your family from last year is going to go. And if he goes, his family goes. Everything is disrupted. Knowing that, I got a good reception. Two things helped me. That year, the roster limit went from 36 to 38. So I was quick to point out that I wasn't taking a spot. There were two new spots and I was taking those.

The 36 guys were safe, although that's not how it turned out. No. 2, Lionel [Aldridge] and Marvin [Fleming] had been there earlier, and Marvin was a little different guy. They pinpointed Marvin to take the brunt of the stuff instead of me. They got to Marvin like they usually do to a first-round draft choice. It's like a very mild hazing, but they picked on Marvin instead of me.

When I got to [St. Norbert] I was the ninth black guy in camp. And for the whole season, I roomed by myself. I was the odd man and didn't have a roommate. In 1968, when we had the strike, Vince said, "We don't have any racial problems in Green Bay." I said to Vince, "We don't have any racial problems because we're winning. If we were losing, all these little things would be magnified." He said, "Like what?" I said, "For example, when I came in as the ninth guy, I roomed by myself on a 38-man roster. That meant somewhere there was a white boy by himself rather than having us room together." I said, "All the way through college, I roomed with the other end who was Dick Anderson, who is still at Penn State coaching and who was white. Then I come to Green Bay and, all of a sudden, rather than put me with a white boy, I was in a room by myself." Vince said, "We'll straighten that out." He went home, back to Green Bay, changed the policy. The first two guys to room together were [Jerry] Kramer and Davis. That was for the 1968 season. [Lombardi] was the general manager, not the coach then. He said, "We did it like that because it had always been done that way." He said he didn't want to make any changes. I said, "I understand coach, but if we were losing, people would be saying 'blah, blah, blah.'" Then all the new guys coming in, it was no longer by race. It was by alphabetical order or something. That was not a major thing, but it could have turned into a major thing if we hadn't been winning.

(During a league-wide labor dispute that delayed the start of training camp in 1968, Robinson was the Packers' player representative and Lombardi was part of NFL management's negotiating team).

[Lombardi] listened and if his thoughts were wrong, he was very open-minded. Now, if you tried to B.S. him, that didn't work.

As a rookie, we went down to Willie & Jim's Tiny Tap Tavern. That was the rookie bar. We weren't allowed to go with the veterans. We'd go in there and they had like Happy Hour and we got like 10-cent beers or nickel beers, real small drafts. All the rookies met there. Then it was like a point of honor [the second year] and you could go with the veterans. Then you didn't want to be seen with the rookies. You were a veteran.

(The Tiny Tap, at that time, was located at 338 Main Ave. in West De Pere.)

I was never a big beer drinker. When I came to Green Bay, the only time I could drink beer was on a very hot day and the beer had to be very cold. For some reason in July, it always went up to like 100 degrees. They were very hot days. We had two-a-days and the beer was always cold. And I drank a little beer then.

Like I said, I played in the All-Star Game. When I got to [the Packers'] camp, [Lombardi] was showing film of that game. There was one reel and everybody was in the meeting room. He was trying to show people how bad they looked in the All-Star Game. I had one play that I thought was my great play. I shed Ron Kramer and made a tackle on Tom Moore for about a three-yard loss. Vince stopped the film right there and I thought I was going to get a little pat on the back. He says, "Kramer! Look at that. That kid there is a rookie and he got rid of you and made the tackle. And he probably won't make the team that he's going to." All the players knew who I was. I wore No. 86 in the All-Star Game. All the players are going, "Vince knows that." Or at least they thought he did. Willie Wood turns around to me and says, "Hey, don't buy a house."

(The All-Stars beat the Packers, 20-17, in 1963.)

At the All-Star Game, the first week, they told me I was going to play defensive end. I worked out with the defensive ends for about two or three days. Your club, your team called [the coaches] in the All-Star Game and told them where to play you. Then [the Packers] called down and they moved me to tight end. I played there about a week. Then they called and they moved me to linebacker finally. Now, before I went to camp, Phil Bengtson had already given me the linebacker book and told me they wanted me to play linebacker. So I was confused playing defensive end and offensive end. When I got to camp [at St. Norbert] I found out what happened. With Bill Quinlan gone, they wanted a defensive end and had gotten Urban Henry and he wasn't what they had in mind. Then Lionel started looking good at defensive end and he became the starter. When they moved me to tight end, they needed a backup for Ron Kramer. Then Marv Fleming started looking good and they moved me to linebacker.

Vince came to me [when I got to camp] and said, "Dave, I don't want you to take it as though I didn't want you as a linebacker. I always thought you'd be a fine linebacker. Phil says he wants you to play linebacker. But we wanted to look at you at other positions." He said, "And our No. 1 concern this year is to win our third consecutive world championship." They had won it in '61 and '62. I didn't know it, but Vince told me, "There are no black linebackers in the National Football League." He said, "We don't need any distractions." There might be reporters writing articles about breaking the color barrier. He said, "If anybody asks you about being the first black linebacker, don't answer them. Tell them to see me and I'll take care of it." That was at St. Norbert. That was the first or second week I was there. I was struggling to play linebacker and he told me, "Don't worry about it. If anybody has any questions, tell them to see me and I'll take care of it." He did.

That wasn't a major concern for me. I was worried about making the team at any position. But he wanted to let me know that they had moved me around down there [at the College All-Star camp] because they wanted to see what I could do and he didn't want any publicity about a black linebacker.

The AFL had them [black linebackers]. But not the NFL. There was one guy who played linebacker, Ted Bates from Oregon who played with St. Louis, but he was a journeyman. He wasn't a starter and I think they finally moved him from linebacker to defensive end or something. That was it. The thinking at the time was that black guys weren't sharp enough to play linebacker.

I was a backup [in 1963]. I played behind [Bill] Forester. If Forester or [Dan] Currie went down, I would have played left or right linebacker. Either one. If [Ray] Nitschke went down, Forester would move into the center and I'd play right linebacker. On Thanksgiving Day, my rookie year, Nitschke broke his arm and was out for the season. I started from Thanksgiving Day on and Forester played the middle.

Lionel and I used to call the pizza place and have them deliver pizzas. We'd open the windows at Sensenbrenner and the [delivery] guy would hand us up the pizza. We were on the first floor and we'd throw money at him. That was the second or third year. My rookie year I was upstairs. We'd leave the windows open because there was no air conditioning in Sensenbrenner and he'd go, "Pizza man, pizza man." The pizza was like five bucks. He'd hand us up the pizza and we'd throw him $10 and tell him to keep the change. We'd have pizza late at night. We had a ball. We were like 21, 22 years old. You know when you're 21, 22, you can eat all the time. There was a phone in the hall. You could make calls because you could make calls to your family. And Lionel would stop by ahead of time and tell them, "Send over a pizza. Triple sausage, triple cheese." And the delivery guy loved us. A $5 tip was big money in those days.

Vince was very tight about your weight. Every Thursday, we'd weigh in and if you were overweight, he'd charge us $10 a pound, which was a lot of money back in 1963. He wanted me at 240 and I couldn't get to 240, so I ate all I could eat. And he wanted Lionel at 245. Lionel was like me about 239, 240. So all the guys would be dieting, and Lionel and I could eat all we wanted to.

Bob Brown, I'm going to tell you, at 269 or below was one of the finest defensive tackles I ever saw in my life. When he got to 279, 280, he got too slow. So Vince got on him and Vince stayed on Bob Brown to lose the weight. Bob wasn't there my first year. He was behind me. But Bob was phenomenal. He couldn't afford barbells, so he'd take two big vegetable cans, maybe 48 ounces, and fill them with concrete and then put a lead pipe between them to make his own barbell to do curls with. I don't know how much it weighed, but I picked it up one time and it was heavy. He'd sit there in front of his bed and do curls all night. Bob was a strong man. He'd do that at St. Norbert. Every year. He'd carry it in, take it up to his room, set it on his bed and do curls.

(Brown played defensive tackle for the Packers from 1966 to 1973.)

Talk about getting fined. We had a rookie—I think it was a tight end from Northwestern. We used to come to camp on Sunday and we'd get Wednesday off, but not the first Wednesday we were in camp. The second Wednesday. So it would be like 10 days before we got a night off. The second Wednesday comes around and everybody's saying, "Tonight's the night, tonight's the night." All the rookies are saying, "What do you mean?" Well, "Tonight after dinner there is no curfew. So go downtown, find yourself a young lady and have her drive you back to St. Norbert. Have her park in the parking lot and as soon as they have check-in at 11 o'clock, go on out. Everybody does it." Of course, nobody does it because they'd be stricter that night than any night. So we all go in and everybody has their windows open because there is no air conditioner.

By 11:15, 11:20, we hear this guy walking down the sidewalk, "Click, click, click." Everybody runs to the window to look to see who it was. Here's this guy dressed to the nines, going down to meet this girl back in the parking lot. We're all laughing. We come in the next day and Vince says, "We had a little incident last night. We had a guy try to sneak out of here." He says, "Rookie, that's going to cost you $300." Max turns to Paul and says, "Three-hundred dollars. That ain't bad. I'm going to get a girl, too." That's what led to Max's famous, "I'm out of here" [line]. Vince says, "He was a rookie. You're a veteran. It's going to cost you $500. And the next guy who leaves this camp it's going to cost $1,000." And that's when he said, "If you find anything worth $1,000 take me with you." Max goes out again and it costs him $1,000. Vince says, "Max, what do you have to say now?" Max says, "Coach, you should have been with me." That's a long story, but that's how it happened. It started with an innocent prank against a rookie. He walked out and right into the trap.

ZEKE BRATKOWSKI

Bratkowski was acquired on waivers from the Los Angeles Rams halfway through the 1963 season and served as Bart Starr's ever reliable backup for the remainder of the Lombardi era. Bratkowski was in his eighth year when the Packers obtained him and he played six more after that. He also served as an assistant coach with the Packers from 1969 to 1970 and again from 1975 to 1981. He was inducted into the Packers Hall of Fame in 1989.

It was a perfect campus for training camp. Everything was close by. One of the problems we had until they built the new hall [Victor McCormick] was that it wasn't air-conditioned. That was a story in itself. Bob Skoronski and I were roommates and we had a fan in the window that had no screen over it. It was just a fan and a blade, and it probably could have flown some airplanes it was so big. And it made enough noise. But those kinds of things, we put up with then. We had all our meetings downstairs and, again, there was no air conditioning. So it would get a little sticky down there in the evenings.

There was a chapel downstairs at Sensenbrenner Hall and Coach Lombardi was down there every morning. It was kind of neat to have that right there in the dorm. I tried to go every day. There weren't very many. [Lombardi] served Mass. We all know how religious he was and how often he spoke about a particular saying in the Bible for his talks. He was there every day.

We used to walk to breakfast together. We'd talk football or whatever. Other guys would walk along with us. It was kind of neat. He didn't have his coaching hat on is probably the best way to say it. It wasn't too far [a walk]. He was very family-oriented. It wasn't just to me. He'd ask, "When is your family coming? Get them here. You need to have your family here." Or he might talk about a preseason game. It varied. And there was an elderly couple that lived there on campus. His name was Ed. He'd be sitting out there on a chair and Coach Lombardi would stop and talk to him. "Ed, how you doing?" All the players did, too. They'd get on him and tease him. [He lived] across the street as you came out of Sensenbrenner. You'd go across the street to where the cafeteria was and we'd walk by him. He'd be sitting out by his garage in a chair and everybody made sure they'd speak to him. He loved that. His garage door was so close to the sidewalk, he couldn't have been more than five yards from us as we walked by. He was there every day. He knew everybody by name.

The rookies had to sing for dinner and there would be a lot of nuns over on the other side of the dining hall who could see these guys. I think they kind of felt sorry for the rookies for the way they were treated. So Fuzzy would fall back on Elijah Pitts. Elijah had a magnificent voice. Elijah would get up on a chair and say, "I'm Elijah Pitts from Philander Smith." And he'd start singing. Well, the veterans knew the song so we'd start humming. And a lot of times the nuns would start humming over there and it was like being in a cathedral because of the beautiful voices they had.

I would say 25, 30 guys went [to Century Lanes]. There'd be nobody in there and we'd go in and the guy would have all the mugs lined up on the bar with these small ice cubes. Everybody drank beer with ice cubes because it was so hot. We just needed a thirst quencher. He'd start pouring that beer and we were on our honor. At the end, we'd say, "We gotta go. It's time for dinner." And we'd just put on the bar how much we felt we drank. There'd be a big stack of money on that bar. In that bar, if you go in the door—unless they've done something—all the signatures are on the wall. It was the front door. As soon as you walked in, they were on the left side. Everybody signed for the owner with like a felt-tip pen.

(The signatures are still there, although they are now encased. The players started signing the plaster wall in 1968, the year Lombardi was general manager. On the wall are the autographs of seven of the players from the Lombardi era who are in the Pro Football Hall of Fame.]

One of the best things that happened there involved Lee Roy Caffey, Tommy Joe Crutcher and, I believe, Donny Anderson. There was a pool table by the bar and they'd play pool when they went in there. They called it, "Texas against the world." There was a restaurant in the back then and one Friday these nuns came in through the bar to go back there and eat. Lee Roy Caffey was poised to make a shot and this was like scripted out of a movie. It was beautiful. A nun walks by—a rosy-cheeked gal with her habit on—and she says, "Mr. Caffey are you going to shoot that shot?" He was leaning over getting ready to shoot and he looks up and said, "Yes, I am." She said, "Well, that's the wrong shot." He stepped back, walked over and gave her the pool cue. She went and chalked the stick up, went to another shot and slammed it in the hole. She said, "That's the shot you should have shot." And then she went to dinner. Everybody got on Caffey, "Boy, you really know how to play that game."

We had two buses that went from St. Norbert to the stadium every day—a.m. and p.m. practices. You could not drive your car there. So there was a veterans' bus and a rookies' bus. They had different veterans driving the bus. Henry Jordan was the bus driver for the rookies. And Bart and I and the quarterbacks always had to catch the first bus. Jimmy Taylor appointed himself to be the driver of the second bus. He'd drive over by Sensenbrenner Hall and start tooting the horn to wake up the veterans to go to practice. [In the afternoon], they'd be rubbing their eyes—they'd be napping. It was about a five-mile ride. Then after practice, they'd be yelling, "First bus is leaving." That meant all you beer drinkers better get on there because they were going back to Sensenbrenner to get in cars and go across the river to Century Lanes. Anyway, Jimmy was driving the bus and they had governors on them. It could only go so fast. Jimmy jumped out of the seat and ran to the back of the bus. He wanted to see who was going to be chicken enough to get that steering wheel. By the time he took two steps, somebody else jumped in behind the controls. Coach Lombardi found out about it and he really ripped into the whole group. And then he appointed bus drivers he could trust.

(Several players told that story or a similar one about Taylor leaving the driver's seat and running down the aisle as the bus was moving. But Jim Maes, who drove the buses and whose family owned the buses, said that wouldn't have been possible. He said there was no cruise control on the buses, so someone would have had to be pressing the accelerator or it would have quickly slowed down. He said on a crowned road the bus also would have veered to the right.)

We usually had our quarterback meetings at the stadium. That's why we had to catch the early bus. We'd meet with [Lombardi] about what we were inserting as far as plays. When we played preseason games, we'd start to get a feel for the game plan before the whole team got it. It was basically team meetings [at St. Norbert].

After the 1965 championship game, I got my first ring. All the other guys had rings from 1961 and '62. It was the day we were supposed to report to training camp for the 1966 season and I came in the locker room to check on the time for my physical. Max had already gotten his physical and he said, "Let's go play golf at Mystery Hills." I said, "Great. Let's go." I had seen Coach Lombardi in the locker room and he had said to me, "What do you think of that championship ring?" Everything was like, "The one I got you." It was always his team and "I got you these rings." I said, "Coach, I love it. I'm really proud to have it. It means a lot to me." So we go play golf and I put the ring and my watch in my left pocket. I noticed Max took his championship ring and watch and wallet and put it in an open compartment on the golf cart. So we play golf, finish up and I reach in my pocket and there's my watch, but no ring. I look in my golf bag, I can't find it. I start going, "Where could I have left that thing?" Well, I could not find it and I was sick. We went back to St. Norbert to eat dinner and we had a meeting. I think Max told Coach Lombardi about me losing my ring, but he didn't say anything. I lied in bed that night and I'll bet I didn't sleep a half-hour. I went over every hole, where I could have taken my watch out. The next day, I'm at breakfast and I must have had bags under my eyes two feet long. Coach Lombardi comes in, walks up to me and says, "I know how much you appreciated your ring, so I went out to Mystery Hills last night with a flashlight and I found your ring." He pulls my championship ring out. He had it in his hand. I said, "How did you find it?" He said, "I can't lie to you. You were playing in front of the man who ran the bookstore at St. Norbert and it was on the fringe of a green and he saw a glint and went over and picked it up." I'll tell you what, I couldn't have been happier.

(Mystery Hills is now Ledgeview Golf Course. The late Larry Berner was manager of the bookstore at the time and also a math professor at St. Norbert.)

I remember once, [Lombardi] yelled down the hall, "Zeke, get down here." I thought, "Oh brother!" He said, "You haven't signed your contract yet." I said, "Nobody gave me one yet." He said, "What do you want?" I said, "I don't know." This was in training camp. He said, "Well, this is what I'll give you." I said, "OK." It was a little bit of a raise and we didn't get big raises. It was maybe mid-20s [for a salary].

TOM BROWN

Drafted by the Packers in the second round in 1963, Brown chose to sign a pro baseball contract and played in 61 games that summer for the Washington Senators. Brown quit baseball less than two weeks before the Packers began training camp a year later and signed to play football. He took over as a starting safety as a rookie and held the position for all five years that he played with the Packers. He was traded to the Washington Redskins in 1969 and played one game for them.

I met Coach Lombardi on the steps of Sensenbrenner Hall the first day. I had just left baseball with the York White Roses in the Washington Senators' organization. I told Coach Lombardi I'd make a decision by July 1. So I said, "OK." He said, "We'll send you a plane ticket and we'll see you at training camp." They were making a film, *Run to Daylight*, with Howard Cosell. He was there and they were filming some stuff, and that's where I met [Lombardi]—on the steps. He said, "Well, we finally got you."

Some of [the filming for *Run to Daylight*] was done on campus; some over at the Packer training facility. I think they filmed the meetings and Cosell was taping the show. He wasn't quite as well known as when he started doing *Monday Night Football*. But Lombardi liked Cosell because Cosell was from New York.

A lot of guys didn't like to get up for breakfast, but we had to go even if you just went over there and showed up. If you didn't go, you were fined. I can remember crossing paths [with Lombardi]. Sometimes I'd say, "Hi, coach." And he wouldn't say anything to you. I'd go, "What the hell did I do now?" But he was in such deep thought, he didn't know you were there. He didn't see you even though you passed within two feet of him. That came out later. Guys would say, "He wasn't friendly to me." But he just didn't know you were going by because he was thinking about something.

I never went to Century Lanes. I wasn't a beer drinker. I think I just went back and watched the news. After the meetings at night or on Wednesday we'd have the night off and a lot of times we'd walk down to De Pere to an A&W root beer [stand] or something. And there was a movie theater on the other side of the bridge. I'd go to the movies once or twice and just relax. It was a quaint little town.

Not one time as long as I played up there did Lombardi come to a [defensive] film session after a game, at training camp, either. I don't think he even came in the defensive meetings. He'd always be at the team meeting. And he'd always start the meeting and have something to say. But then we'd always break up. The defensive team went to another room. But he never ever critiqued a film with the defense at St. Norbert. You have to understand that the defense, at that time, was pretty well set. He did everything with the offense and Phil Bengtson did everything with the defense. [Bengtson] was opposite of Lombardi: very matter of fact, this is the way it's going to be. He was really a great coach, great insight. He'd go over the tendencies of the other team, then told us the type of defense we'd play. I remember him being a chain smoker: one Camel after another.

I wasn't up there when Lombardi smoked. He had stopped smoking by then.

The rookies had to put on a play at the end of training camp. It wasn't much fun. [But Lombardi] didn't mind you making fun of him. There was one guy who would always play Lombardi. [Lombardi would] laugh as hard as anybody else. That was a great time, although some years were better than others. It would be about things that happened during training camp, on the field, where he'd holler at people, sayings that he had. That's what it was. It wasn't [an actual] play. The rookies had to put that on, but there weren't many rookies left at the end of training camp. The guy playing Lombardi would pretend he was hollering at the players and everybody would laugh because it was funny.

DOUG HART

Hart played eight years with the Packers, starting at cornerback in 1965 and at safety from 1969 to 1971. Hart originally signed with the Packers in 1963 after he had been cut by the St. Louis Cardinals and spent the season on the taxi squad.

The normal day, we'd go to breakfast I think about 7:30. We'd be at the stadium about 9:30, on the field at 10, off the field about 11:30. We'd be back at St. Norbert for lunch. The first two weeks, we'd have 3:30 in the afternoon workouts and that's when we had to jam the time in to get the beer. But once we had gotten through the first two weeks, we didn't have the afternoon practice. So a lot of guys would just lie around in bed. Carroll Dale and I would run over and play nine holes of golf at Mystery Hills. The club over there would be all set up for us. They'd have our cart out and ready, and all we had to do was get our bags out of the car, walk over and put them on the cart and go play nine holes. Carroll and I would get on the first bus, get back and go right through the lunch line. We'd eat and quickly get in a car and drive across [to the course].

The bus would stop at the dormitory [in the afternoon], we'd all get out and jump in our cars and go across the bridge to the bowling alley, Century Lanes. That's where they had the most wonderful beer glasses. All the glasses would be in the freezer and they'd put the beer in it and it would form crystals. It would really cool you down. There were a number of us: easily 15 to 20 guys each time. Jerry [Kramer]. Max McGee would be there sometimes. Paul Hornung would be there. And as we went through the years, guys like Donny Anderson and Jim Grabowski went there, too. It was just sort of a traditional thing. It would be about 5 o'clock in the evening and we'd have one hour. I don't know about Buck's. We had a time period, so it would be only 30, 35 minutes, maybe 40 minutes, that we'd be there. You could get three of them down. [The beer] was so cold, it would damn near freeze your throat. All we wanted was to get those beers down us.

We'd go back to the cafeteria, get our tray and start pointing at food that you wanted to eat. You wouldn't get loopy, but you'd be affected. It wasn't much. Never [did Lombardi say anything]. He knew it was going on. He knew we were there and what we were doing. There was never a problem with it.

The only time fans were [around St. Norbert] was following preseason games. We'd have friends and relatives and everybody would eat Jell-O. That was our nickname: "Jell-O dinners." They had all kinds of Jell-O for the players. It was a cafeteria style affair and they thought Jell-O was good for the players and their recovery. There was a meal, but also a lot of Jell-O.

KEN BOWMAN

A product of the University of Wisconsin, Bowman was drafted by the Packers in the eighth round in 1964. He took over as the starting center during his rookie year, but two years later he injured his shoulder in the preseason and played in only four games. Bowman got his job back in Super Bowl I, following the 1966 season, when he replaced an injured Bill Curry and started for most of the next seven seasons. He played with the Packers from 1964 to 1973 and was inducted into the Packers Hall of Fame in 1981.

I went to the All-Star Game down in Chicago. I got back to Packer camp probably about August 8 or 9. There was me, Lloyd Voss, Dennis Claridge and Tommy Joe Crutcher. I can't tell you who greeted us. I don't think they made any big deal. We came into camp. Lombardi had his meeting after supper, and he acknowledged that we had arrived in camp.

[Lombardi] was a very forceful speaker, a very forceful man. Yeah, he left an impression that this was the coach. Somebody once asked me if any of the players ever called Coach Lombardi, "Vinnie." I said,

"That would be like calling Attila the Hun, Tillie." If you didn't want your head handed to you, you treated him with respect. And, by and large, he treated most of the players with respect. He addressed [us] as "Gentlemen." I guess the impression I got from the initial meeting was that we were a cut above the rest of the league. We are the Green Bay Packers. [We] were expected to win, expected to conduct ourselves in such a way that befitted a champion.

I remember one time right after I got there—I was playing center and Bob Skoronski was playing center, too—I was kind of tagging along after "Ski" to learn assignments and things. So Ski and I headed down to a place called The Dairy Bar and got a double-dip cone before dinner. Coach Lombardi and the rest of the coaches used to get together and had a 5 o'clock club down in one of the rooms at Sensenbrenner Hall. Then they'd come over for dinner. So Ski and I are walking along in front of the student union with our ice cream cones and here comes Lombardi from across the street. "Good evening, boys." I said, "Good evening," and I'm slopping down my ice cream cone. I look at Skoronski and say, "Where the hell is your cone?" He said, "I threw it in the bush back there." You're talking about a guy who had been there about six years and that kind of showed me the fear a lot of the players had for Lombardi.

I started out with Lloyd Voss [as a roommate]. He was the No. 1 draft choice in 1964. He got traded to Pittsburgh and then I got Travis [Williams]. That was a trip. He'd walk in the room and he was so full of B.S. He'd say, "Sammm," my nickname. Don't ask me why, but Lombardi called me, "Sam." [Williams would go] "Sammm, Sam, Sam, wild rumors are circulating that you are a bigoted, biased man. But I discounted them immediately upon hearing them. I knew a man of your social stature could ill afford such a violent, base reputation." I can still give it to you word for word. He was loaded with a bunch of these garbage sayings. He was a good roomie, though.

I remember Lombardi had Travis holding a ball over there [at St. Norbert]. Travis fumbled a couple times and Lombardi had him carry a football wherever he went. [Williams] would go over to the Union to eat and set his ball down like it was his little baby. Had to carry it to meetings, had to be with him at all times. He didn't particularly like it and he was eager to show that he didn't need the ball anymore. So he was sure as hell not going to fumble again. It was for a week, maybe two.

CARROLL DALE

After playing the first five years of his career with the Los Angeles Rams, Dale was traded to the Packers in 1965 and immediately took over as a starting wide receiver. He was the Packers' deep threat when they won three straight NFL titles from 1965 to 1967 and averaged 19.7 yards a catch over his entire eight years with the team. He played his final season with the Minnesota Vikings in 1973. Dale was inducted into the Packers Hall of Fame in 1979.

When two-a-days were over, every once in awhile, we'd have an afternoon off, so we'd sneak out [and go golfing]. [We went to] Mystery Hills; Shorewood [too] because it was away from camp.

We had an afternoon one day and went over to Shorewood. I was close to a tree and I said to Doug [Hart], "What happens if I hit this tree?" He was sitting on the cart and he said, "I don't know. It probably will bounce." So, sure enough, I hit this little tree and the ball came back and hit him on the lip, his upper lip just below his nose. There was blood flying. I lived on John Street, across from East River Park. So we went by the house and tried to put a butterfly on it. It swelled up and that didn't help it much, so we tried to figure out what we were going to say. Coach [Red] Cochran asked Doug about it and he said, "We were standing on the street corner and a truck came by with one of those mirrors sticking out and it hit me in the mouth." That was training camp. That was the worst thing about it. They gave us time off to rest and we were out playing golf. I wasn't with Doug when Red asked him that, but it was back at camp at night.

I knew who [Lombardi] was. I had seen him on TV. I guess my attitude was great when I got there because I was leaving a team that had had five losing seasons and I knew, at least, that we were a

116

contender. So my attitude was one of gratitude that he had traded for me. I was so thankful to be there, I wasn't about to jeopardize that.

[Lombardi's] opening speeches at St. Norbert always included that there should be only three things on our mind. No. 1, your church, God or religion. No. 2, your family. No. 3, Green Bay Packer football and nothing else. He gave that speech every year.

I roomed with Ray Nitschke all the years [that Lombardi was there]. Ray was very considerate and I tried to be considerate of him. He went to bed early. So we got along fine. Have you heard me tell the story about going down to an exhibition game in Milwaukee and staying at the Pfister? Ray, at St. Norbert, like I said, would go to bed early and get up during the night and go down the hall to the restroom. At the Pfister, we stayed in the towers and there were 16 rooms in a circle. Ray had already gone to bed about 9:30 or 10, and I was watching TV. Ray gets up to go to the restroom. Usually, about 11, it was bed-check time and the coaches would come around. So I heard a knock on the door and I waited. I thought Ray was in the restroom and he ought to be about through and he could just open the door and speak to the coaches. Then I heard a knock on the door again. Finally, I get up and go to the door and there's Ray standing out in the hall. What happened was that Ray thought he was at St. Norbert. The bad thing about being at the Pfister was that Ray slept in the nude. So he had been out in the hall wondering around for two, three minutes stark naked. I lied down on the bed laughing and he goes, "What are you laughing about? You better not tell anybody." I didn't until the next morning.

BILL CURRY

Curry was drafted by the Packers as a future—a senior who had redshirted and had a year left of college eligibility—in the 20th round of the 1964 draft, but he couldn't sign with them until the following year. Curry played only two seasons with the Packers, but started at center in 1966 when they won the NFL championship. He was selected by New Orleans in the 1967 expansion draft and traded to the Baltimore Colts,

*where he played six years before finishing his career with one-year stints
with the Houston Oilers and Los Angeles Rams. Curry started for the
Colts for five years, including the year they won Super Bowl V. He also
served as offensive line coach of the Packers from 1977 to 1979.*

I had a traumatic experience for a kid that age. I was really just a
baby. I was 22 years old, but I had never been out of Georgia. I
didn't understand much of anything about anything. And, here, I'm
reporting to this different environment. When I say different, I can't
tell you culturally how big a difference.

I was to report from the College All-Star Game, so I get on an
airplane with Junior Coffey and we're to fly from Chicago to Green
Bay. He's the other rookie. We get to Milwaukee and a flight atten-
dant comes up to us and says, "One of you has to get off because there
was a mistake in the reservations back there." It ended up that I was
the one designated to get off. I walk in and see that it's now about
noon and I'm supposed to be in De Pere, Wis., at 4:30. The guy smiles
and says, "Fine, we'll put you on the next plane out of here, which is
tomorrow morning." I went ballistic. I was terrified. I was going to
be late to my first meeting with Vince Lombardi. So I bravely call for
the station manager of North Central Airlines. He comes out and he's
just trying to get me from the counter—you could tell. He keeps
saying, "I'm very sorry. It was just a mistake in the reservations
process. These things happen. You'll be OK."

Well, I didn't have a credit card. Cell phones didn't exist. I wouldn't
have known how to rent a car. So I was in easy reach of the training
camp, but couldn't get there. In desperation I finally said, "Give me your
name and give me your position with the company. I'm supposed to
report to Vince Lombardi this afternoon and I'm going to be late."
His whole demeanor changed. He said, "Hold on one minute." He
walked out from behind the counter, had my bags pulled off the big
plane and he chartered a single-engine plane and flew me to
Manitowoc. A North Central van met me at Manitowoc and I walked
in at 4:15. Went straight to campus, straight to where "The Man" was
waiting for me just inside the door at Sensenbrenner Hall. I've never felt

such a sense of relief in my life. People have a hard time believing that story, but it was my first brush with the Lombardi mystique. He looked me in the eye and said, "Are you ready to go to work now?" I gave the only answer, "Yes sir." I had memorized my lines.

It was the night of the intra-squad scrimmage. The first thing we did was to go over to Lambeau Field and get ready for the scrimmage. [Lombardi] walked up in front of the team and that was the first time I had been in a team setting with him, and he said the field was "inundated." I think that's the first time I ever heard the word inundated, so I filed that to go look it up. But it was raining cats and dogs, and he said, "We're going to go scrimmage anyhow." I think I remember most everything he said when I was with him.

I have especially fond memories [of St. Norbert] because I was a theology student in my second year with the Packers at Candler School of Theology at Emory University in Atlanta. Candler agreed to accept credits from St. Norbert as long as I didn't take theology, as long as I took sociology and psychology. So I took a full load on the St. Norbert campus in the fall of 1966, at the same time I was playing for the Packers. That allowed me to continue my work at Candler and at the same time stay out of the service. Also, Coach Lombardi was very cooperative. My draft status was changed. So I attended three, three-hour classes over there that whole fall. It was structured in the afternoon, so I never had to miss practice or meetings. The work was fairly difficult, but I enjoyed it so much it wasn't onerous. As I recall I was through with the Packers about mid-afternoon and that's when I went to class.

During training camp, I was so exhausted that between practices I didn't go anywhere. I was not a beer drinker, so I wasn't part of the 5 o'clock club, as they affectionately called themselves. I just enjoyed my Spartan surroundings and tried to rest between practices and at night after meetings.

I never liked training camp anywhere now that I mention it. It wasn't St. Norbert that I didn't like. It was two-a-days and constant football meetings. I never enjoyed all of that until I became a coach. Now, I think it's great. When I was a player, I didn't think it was so cool. So I remember it being a very Spartan place and the students were never there. The time I enjoyed it most was with the other students, when they were on campus in the fall of '66. That was fun. Training camp was not a fun time to me. It was a very stressful time, especially when I was with the Packers and was clearly outmanned by everybody there.

[Lombardi's presence] was overwhelming to me. Heck, I had to write a book to right the ship. I didn't respond well to Coach Lombardi. I'm not proud of that, so I've written a book in which I tell the whole story. Eventually, I went to see him at Georgetown Hospital five years later. The book is *Ten Men You Meet in the Huddle.* I was utterly unglued by him. Even when he got with me personally, which he did, and taught me—and he was an incredible teacher—I couldn't get past the mystique and the fact he was so different from anybody I ever worked for. I just didn't handle any of it very well. Very demanding. Very tough time for me. It was mostly my fault. It was mostly my immaturity that was the problem.

I was always the smallest lineman. I was supposed to stuff myself [at the training table], but I couldn't eat much because I was too uptight. I played at about 235. Never in my career did I play over 245. And it took me years and years to get to 240. [Lombardi] told me the first day, "I'd like you to gain about 10 pounds." So I did, but it took me about 10 years, five years. I could hardly choke [the food] down I was so uptight.

Most of the interaction with the guys was on the bus going and coming, or at Lambeau Field. In the meeting rooms, it was strictly business. So there wasn't much horseplay. I remember we had the rookie show over in the dining hall on campus; the infamous rookie show in which Donny Anderson took out $1 bills and lit them up. They were real dollars and Coach Lombardi was not amused at all. [Anderson] was spoofing his contract. He was the richest guy ever in the NFL. [Lombardi] just scowled. After every act, after every part of every act, all eyes turned to Vince to see if he approved. Usually, he'd just laugh and slap his knee no matter how ridiculous the deal was. But he was not happy with Donny.

DONNY ANDERSON

Anderson was drafted by the Packers in the first round of the 1965 draft as a future and also was a first-round pick by the Houston Oilers of the American Football League in a special redshirt draft. At the time, the two leagues were competing for players; thus, Anderson, a Texas native and product of Texas Tech, became the object of a fierce bidding war the following year when he became eligible to turn pro. Anderson, designated by Lombardi to be Paul Hornung's heir apparent at halfback, signed a contract worth more than $700,000, an unheard of sum at the time. In the 1966 NFL draft, the Packers selected fullback Jim Grabowski in the first round and gave him a $400,000 deal to be Jim Taylor's replacement. Thus, when the two reported to camp in the summer of '66, they literally composed "The Million Dollar Backfield." Anderson played six years with the Packers before he was traded to the St. Louis Cardinals for MacArthur Lane. Anderson was inducted into the Packers Hall of Fame in 1983.

Jim Grabowski was my roommate for five years in training camp. Lombardi addressed [the contracts]. He said [they were done] to compete and to stay competitive and to beat the up-and-coming AFL— he made that statement to the team. I'm not exactly sure when he told everybody that. But it was pretty well taken and I don't remember much harassment at all. Looking back, there could have been some envy by some of the players because we weren't proven. Mine was $720,000, I think. I'm not sure what Grabo's was, but I think it was $400,000-plus.

Being a Texas boy, one of the things that was a little strange [at St. Norbert] was not having air conditioning. Some of the guys had fans. The second part was just being a rookie and being [treated] different in that once you parked your car, you couldn't drive it during the day to practice. It was a Lombardi rule and I understood it. We rode a bus instead of having 100 [players] driving their cars. Lombardi had curfews, so we had to be in by 11 o'clock. That was kind of a bummer, [although] Lombardi was good about letting guys have time off.

We did a skit right before we broke training camp where Grabo and I were tipping people when we traveled. We got some play money: $100 bills. We were tipping one hundreds, walking around and puffing on cigars. As I recall, Lombardi laughed at it. All the rookies who made the team—there were eight of us—just did a little skit. We were passing out $100 bills to butlers, valet people. It was just fun.

The first meeting I went to all the veterans were kind of sitting in the back. They knew to get there maybe five minutes early; I got there four minutes early and most of the seats were taken. Vince started screaming and hollering about something. He wasn't very happy for whatever reason. It probably didn't have anything to do with anything other than that he wanted to let Grabowski and me know he was the boss.

1966 was the year Lombardi went to $1,000 for [fines]. I don't think there were a lot of guys, when it was about one-fifteenth of their salary, sneaking out. If you were making $15,000, $1,000 was pretty stiff. I think Lombardi got tired of fining people $100, so he made it $1,000.

GALE GILLINGHAM

Gillingham was the second of the Packers' two first-round draft picks in 1966. He took over for Fuzzy Thurston as the starting left guard the following year, Lombardi's last season as coach, and became one of the most dominant offensive linemen in Packers' history. He played from 1966 to 1974 and again in 1976. A five-time Pro Bowl pick, he was inducted into the Packers Hall of Fame in 1982.

It was a long training camp in those days. It was eight or nine weeks every year. It wasn't like it is now. When I first got there, we stayed in an older dorm. There wasn't air conditioning or anything. It was pretty hot. Forrest [Gregg] and I bought a fan. Then it wasn't too bad. My first roommate was Ronnie Rector and he got cut or traded. Then I was with Red Mack. Then for a couple of years, I roomed with Forrest. The beds were small, the rooms were small. But, basically, we were never in the room except for sleeping.

My rookie year, I had a broken hand when I got there. I broke my right hand at [a] College All-Star [practice]. Then they shipped me back [to Green Bay] and I played against the All-Stars. I broke my hand like the first day and Lombardi said, "Get him back here." I took the train up and grabbed a cab to St. Norbert.

I was trying to eat left-handed and they made me get up every night [to sing]. I never got enough to eat until that was over. They didn't have that all the way through training camp. I think they ended that when the exhibition games started. We used to all run out and buy songbooks. Geez! You had to get up there, say your name, be loud. You'd get catcalls. Everybody got the same thing. Donny and Grabo weren't there yet, so they always called for the No. 1 draft pick first. Every night. I was up there every night and there'd probably be five or six of us. And Lombardi was big on that. He wanted to see how we reacted after a good day or bad day at practice. He told us that. So you got up on your chair and made damn sure you spoke loud enough. It didn't make much difference after that because nobody was going to like what you were singing. It was pretty much a joke, but you had to make an attempt or [Lombardi] didn't like that. I was no singer, but I knew what he wanted, so I got up there and told them who I was and where I was from, and was loud.

The food was great. That was the best food I ever had in my entire life: what they had at training camp. One night a week, we'd have prime rib. Good beef. Pretty much anything you wanted. Then after the exhibition games, everybody had to go back to St. Norbert if the game was in town. [Lombardi] would have a banquet there. The reason was—and he told us this—he didn't want a lot of young guys that he didn't know or trust yet running around the streets. But, boy, the spread they put on there was unbelievable. I know my father-in-law and mother-in-law came over a couple times; [my father-in-law] was in shock. They had shrimp. Prime rib. [Lombardi] was there, all the coaches. [Lombardi] would mingle with the guests he had there.

We'd go back to our rooms [after dinner] and then we'd have a meeting in the evening until about 9:30, 10. They'd start about 7. They'd have a short offensive meeting, then split up: linemen, backs, whatever. Except Wednesday, they'd let the married guys go home from dinner until they checked us in [at the dorm]. They checked us every night. They came to every room. On Wednesday, you had off from when dinner was over until 11 o'clock.

We got our ass chewed every night. Whatever point [Lombardi] was trying to get over that night, he'd be harping on something. When we were at [Sensenbrenner], there was a meeting room downstairs. From there, we'd go to position meetings. Offensive linemen would be in one room, backs another. You know the first part of training camp, they were putting in plays. They'd put in what you were going to do the next day. The first thing they'd do is go through the films of the day's practice. They filmed everything. They'd have their coaching points and then you'd go on to your next set of plays.

[Lombardi] was always tough. Yeah! I heard some horrendous ass chewings in those meetings. He never swore. But he did everything but. That's just the way it was.

I think they got us up at 6 o'clock. You'd go right to breakfast and they'd check you in there, too. You had just a few minutes [after breakfast] to get over to the stadium for practice. If you got caught in a car, it was a pretty big fine, which was smart. They didn't want guys running around where you could get in an accident. They were old school buses. Two buses: a first bus and a second bus. In those days, you'd come back to St. Norbert for lunch, then you'd have about an hour and get back on the bus for the afternoon practice. Most of them [napped]. I never could sleep much during the day, so I just sat there.

Bob Brown was always in trouble because he was always overweight. I remember Leon Crenshaw was trying to lose weight at one time and he collapsed at noon. He flopped right down on the floor right at the cafeteria where we ate. They got him and got some liquids back in him. He was losing weight too fast. He was a big guy. I think he was like 300 pounds. I don't remember a fat-man's table. In those days, you either got with it or they got rid of you.

Lombardi's camps, physically, were the easiest. Mentally, they were the worst because he never quit chewing everybody's ass. He was on everybody. Compared to what I did at the University of Minnesota, they were like a holiday, physically. The [head coaches] who came later added stuff: running, oh geez. I'll tell you something: [Lombardi] never did anything that wasn't related to a play that we were going to run outside of his grass drills. And we didn't do that very long, either. Ten days, two weeks. As far as sprints afterward, we never ran any farther than 20 yards. We ran plays into the end zone from the 20-yard line. I came from a place—the U in Minnesota—where you'd hit people just to see if you'd hit them.

[The meetings at St. Norbert] were very intense. [Lombardi] always had his coaching points that had to happen or the play didn't work. Everything he did was football related. But he was so damn intense, everything was intense. You really had to concentrate. It was fairly new to me. He made everything fairly simple, outside of you'd get chewed if you didn't have your foot in the right place. Very simple offense, very easy to remember. That was his thing: Keep it simple, everybody go full speed and everybody do their techniques right, and then things usually work.

JIM FLANIGAN

Flanigan was selected in the second round of the 1967 draft and played four seasons with the Packers, including Lombardi's last season. Flanigan was primarily a backup at middle linebacker. His son, Jim Flanigan, also played for the Packers in 2001.

It was my first training camp, so everything was new. [Lombardi] went to Mass every morning and I was brought up in that same environment. So I'd see him at Mass every morning. He used to serve as the altar boy. There'd be maybe two or three other players, and maybe 10 or 15 people. Zeke Bratkowski was there quite often and Bob Skoronski. [Lombardi] did his part and was very quiet. He helped serve and that was when they had the platter underneath the Eucharist and that's what he did. He got the water and wine.

I was called by Pat Peppler after I was drafted in the second round and told to report to camp. Things were quite different than they are now days. So there was a telephone call, he [Peppler] flew in to deal with my agent, the contract was signed and I drove to St. Norbert from Pennsylvania. I'm sure there was a general session where [Lombardi] introduced himself to everybody. He was a motivational speaker. He was telling you the routine and what was expected of you. That was back when a lot of the veteran players couldn't run a lap around the field. They weren't in any type of condition. That was when training camp was training camp. We were probably the first wave of rookies—or maybe Anderson and Grabowski the year before—who came into training camp fully conditioned.

We had no weight facilities at all. We had one Universal and he [Lombardi] didn't want anybody lifting weights. He wanted us to use those Exer-Genies. He didn't want us to get muscle-bound.

[The dorm] was pretty much like an army barracks. The rooms were small. The bathrooms were for everybody. It was a typical dormitory setting. Some of the veterans would bring their own mattresses because they didn't like the mattresses that were available. They were small, compact, what you'd find in a dormitory. It was two men to a room. You had your breakfast, lunch and dinner [on campus], and you had to attend every meal.

[The players] would go over to the bowling alley. Cold beer and you'd drink as much as you could as fast as you could and go back over for dinner. You were bused back and forth [from practice], but by the time you got back to the dormitory, then you could jump in your car. You'd have maybe a half-hour, 45 minutes by the time you got to the bar. You'd have your first one real fast and then you'd sit and socialize. It wasn't a drunken binge at all. [The veterans] wanted you to participate. They wanted to find out about you. You probably can find out more about somebody in a social setting after a few beers than you do on the field. Once you got into training camp, you were part of the team and they probably could see who was going to make it or who wasn't going to make it. And the guys who showed more promise, they kind of took you under their arm and helped you.

CHAPTER 6

The Media

BUD LEA

Lea covered the Packers for the Milwaukee Sentinel from 1954 to 1972. After leaving the beat, he continued writing about them as a sports editor and columnist at the Sentinel until his retirement in 1995. Since then he has continued to write columns about the Packers for Packer Plus, a weekly magazine published by the Milwaukee Journal Sentinel. Lea is a native of Green Bay.

My folks lived in Green Bay. So when I went up there covering the Packers when[Lisle] Blackbourn and those guys were there, I stayed with them. The paper was so cheap, they didn't pay for hotels or anything, so I stayed with my folks. When Lombardi came in, he said, "You have to stay at Sensenbrenner Hall." I said, "Why?" He said, "That's the way we do it." So I was put on the second floor of Sensenbrenner Hall with the rookies. My roommate was the guy from United Press, Gene Hintz. He snored so much I couldn't sleep. After a couple days, I said, "The hell with this." I just left. Lombardi was so worked up about his team, he didn't even know I had left. I went back to my folks' house.

The other thing was the bathrooms were at the end of the hall. I'm a skinny little guy with these big old football players taking up most of the room. It was really an uncomfortable place.

Did we have curfew? Yeah, 11 o'clock. Lombardi told us, "These are the rules. Abide by curfew just like everybody else in this place. It's not just an open door here at Sensenbrenner. You stay with the team, those are the rules." I wrote my stories there, but then I'd have to go down to Western Union, across the street from the Northland Hotel, to file it. We didn't have computers. You typed your story, went down to Western Union.

You had to go to the 5 o'clock club. Lombardi told us we had to. I was on a morning deadline, but I went there. I thought it would be a chance to relax with these guys, rub shoulders with the coaches. When he first came in, Lombardi started it. But the rules were that everything was off the record. You couldn't talk about any plays or football. Lombardi held court. It was his party. They had drinks down there. You could go and have a drink with the coach. That's where I got to know Cooper Rollow [of the Chicago Tribune]. He didn't have anywhere to go, so we went to the 5 o'clock club. But the media all hung together and the coaches all hung together. It was like two cliques. There was no mixture or anything. And, boy, it would end at five minutes to six. Everybody cleared out. Lombardi was really punctual.

You read David Maraniss' book about how Lombardi was such a cruel son of a bitch to guys like Lee Remmel. I really felt sorry for Lee. He was a mild guy and didn't make any waves. I remember the story when W.C. Heinz was up there working on *Run to Daylight*. I guess Remmel was waiting outside Lombardi's office and Heinz was the only guy allowed in the Packers' coaches' office because he was writing this book. He noticed that Remmel was sitting outside and said, "Somebody is waiting for you." Vince said, "Who is that?" Heinz said, "Lee Remmel." Lombardi says, "What does he want?" Heinz says, "Tell him to come in. Talk to him." Lombardi goes, "I don't want to talk to him." Heinz says, "He has a job. He has a family. He's a good writer. He could work for any paper. He does a good job for the paper here. You treat him like crap."

Anyway, I guess Vince invited Lee to the 5 o'clock club. I remember Lee came in and was a nervous wreck. Vince is saying, "Lee, Lee have a drink." And Lee was on pins and needles. But it was mostly for out-of-town writers. Cooper Rollow. The Chicago Tribune was there a lot because the Packers were so popular. There'd be a wire service guy. Myself. Maybe a visiting writer from New York or somewhere. All the assistant coaches would be there. Tom Miller, Chuck Lane. But as I told you, the coaches hung together and we hung together. They'd have beer there. They'd have Scotch, whiskey. I think Marie called one day. [Lombardi] had gotten so caught up in his football team that he forgot their anniversary. She finally got him at St. Norbert and I guess she said, "Thanks a lot, shithead." God, we loved her.

All Lombardi wanted to do was get Tom Miller to fix his drink, a Scotch and water, and get the paper so he could read the Press-Gazette. And he wanted to watch his television show, including cartoons. He'd watch *Tom & Jerry*, and laugh. We thought he was a weird S.O.B. What's wrong with this genius?

(Miller played two games for the Packers in 1946 and then spent 31 years in their front office. He was publicity director when Lombardi was hired in 1959 and became assistant general manager to him in 1966. When Miller retired he was assistant to the president.)

Lombardi never drank much at the 5 o'clock club. He'd maybe have a couple Scotch and waters. He wasn't a pounder. The pounder was Phil Bengtson. That's the guy who could put them down. Some of the other assistant coaches, too. But Lombardi was the high priest about everything. But nobody was ever kicked out of the 5 o'clock club. Nobody ever got drunk. Nobody ever said anything outrageous. Nobody ever confronted Lombardi.

Lombardi didn't have a room [at Sensenbrenner]. He stayed over at McCormick Hall when he didn't go home. All the veterans were on the first floor at Sensenbrenner. All the rookies and the media were on the second floor. The 5 o'clock club was held in the basement. It was a big room. That was Lombardi's only time to relax. He'd talk about politics, what was in the news. He dominated the conversation. Everybody else would be nodding like yes men. He'd read the Press-Gazette.

I remember the players used to always ask me, "What's the 5 o'clock club? What do you guys do there?" I told them, "Nothing. We just have a drink. It's almost like you're ordered to be there."

[The players] were really afraid of Lombardi. He'd embarrass guys coming through the line. A guy would take too many scoops of ice cream, he'd call him, "Fatso." Belittle the guy. "Put it back, you're too damn fat." Even Bob Skoronski. He was dying for an ice cream after a hot afternoon practice. I guess he went somewhere close to St. Norbert College and got a double-dip. He's sitting on a park bench and Lombardi comes by, and he put the ice cream behind his back. Skoronski was never out of shape, but they were just fearful of the guy.

We were allowed to go in the cafeteria and eat with the Packers. The media would sit at their own table. We'd listen to those guys sing their college songs. [Gale] Gillingham hated it. He'd have to sing the University of Minnesota fight song and he just hated it, hated it.

I remember one time I had an assignment to go up there with a photographer to shoot everything: all the drills, over at St. Norbert College. We could go to St. Norbert then and interview players in their rooms. We did that all the time. Niels Lauritzen was the photographer for this assignment and it was raining like hell. Instead of a big wire fence around the Oneida Street practice field back then there was just a railing around it. The only car on the field was Lombardi's. He drove his car right out on the field. Niels Lauritzen has all this equipment so he drives his car right behind Lombardi's. Vince was so attentive to the drills, he doesn't even see it. But Tom Miller sees it and says, "God, get your car out of here. Please, please, get your car out of here. If he sees that, he's going to be just awful." Lombardi finally sees him and just read Niels out like hell. I felt so sorry for the guy. It was pouring rain. And Vince could easily have gotten his car out. But that wasn't the point. Vince was the only one allowed to drive on that field. He just belittled the hell out of Niels. I remember telling Niels, "Now, when you're finished, you've got to go over to St. Norbert." Niels was a tough guy. He said, "Yeah, I'll go over there." So he set up all his strobe lights at the cafeteria, where the Packers ate their evening meal. Boy, the first guy to come through was Lombardi. He looked at Niels and said, "Oh hell, have dinner with us."

We could go right up to their rooms to interview them. Jerry Kramer was great. Willie Davis. That was when Kramer and Davis were the first black and white roommates. You'd just walk right in their rooms. They'd have their morning practice and then bus back to St. Norbert for lunch. Then they'd go up to their rooms to take a nap before the afternoon drill. But you could go in their rooms and they'd have the freedom to talk to you. They didn't have rules like they have today. In that way, they were very, very open.

LEE REMMEL

Remmel was a sportswriter for the Green Bay Press-Gazette for almost 30 years, writing about the Packers throughout that period. After leaving the paper in 1974, he spent 33 years working for the Packers as public relations and publicity director, and as team historian. He was inducted into the Packers Hall of Fame in 1996 and retired in 2007.

I went to the 5 o'clock club quite a few times in the mid 1960s. Art Daley asked me to replace him on the beat in 1967. I had been there before, but that was when I became a regular, so to speak. It was sometimes tense there. Vince would read the paper quite frequently. In fact, he even quoted me a little bit. He did it on one or two occasions. He always made a comment. He was definitely in charge. He loved watching cartoons on TV and one time at the 5 o'clock club, Tony Canadeo walked by and snapped it off. Lombardi yelled, "Turn that back on. I was watching it." That was at St. Norbert. I think Tony was somewhat of a regular. I can't say he was there every night, but he was on the executive committee and had a reason to be there. I think Dick Bourguignon, who was vice president, was there off and on. I don't have any recollection of Dominic Olejniczak [the president] being there.

Tom Miller kind of served as host. It was a PR thing really and that's what he was, director of public relations.

I can't speak for other people, but I was careful around [Lombardi]. I knew how explosive he could be. But if he ever relaxed, that was when he relaxed. And I don't think he relaxed very much. He had friends from New York who came to the 5 o'clock club.

By quarter to six, people would start working their way over to the dining hall. Excellent food. They had steaks, good desserts, ice cream every night.

Vince wanted the rookies to sing for their supper and he always had somebody in charge of that operation. A guy named Jim Weatherwax was a secretary if you will. He'd arrange the schedule. If the veterans didn't like the singing, they'd yell out, "Wax." Even years after he was gone, they'd still do that. Once in awhile, Vince would interrupt if it became too discordant and yell for Elijah Pitts. Elijah had a strong, but untrained voice. Vince would say, "Elijah, show these guys how to sing." And he'd sing like *Old Man River* or *Trees* or something like that and Vince would beam benevolently and all was right with the world. A defensive back named Howie Williams was another good singer. He'd sing, *San Francisco*. It was in the style of the day. He sang that song very well.

Once in awhile, I'd go over to St. Norbert for an interview. This would be in the dining hall, off to the side. I remember interviewing Paul Hornung out there.

Even though Lombardi was a strict disciplinarian, Hornung and [Max] McGee were confident about getting in and out of training camp. And Vince was human. I remember I noted in a story one year that Max McGee looked a little billowy. Vince said, "I would like to have 22 Max McGees on my football team." I think he liked their skills certainly, but also their confidence. They were two great football players.

DAVE O'HARA

O'Hara was state sports editor in Wisconsin for the Associated Press from 1959 to 1965. He started working for AP as an office boy in 1942 and retired in 1992, except for two years during the Korean War. After leaving Wisconsin, he was based in Boston and was New England sports editor for 27 years. He's currently retired and living in Winter Haven, Fla.

They put me up in a room at the end of the hall [at Sensenbrenner], but it was also near the washrooms. If the fellas were out, they'd have to be back at a certain hour. They'd wait until the assistants were in [and had conducted bed check]. Then they'd tiptoe down to the john and some of them would come in my room for one last beer or something. Oh sure [I had beer in the room]. I just went and bought it and brought it in. I might have had a bottle of booze, too. Don't forget the school was closed. No refrigerator, you had to look for ice. I'd be up [at St. Norbert] for only three days at a time. I'd go up and get a week of stories. I'd work in my room. I was on the first floor. That's where Tom Miller put me. He thought I was out of the way and I was. But between practices and in the early evening, I got several stories. Forrest Gregg, for one. Bill Quinlan and I were very friendly. I found out what room they were in and I'd knock on the door.

The 5 o'clock club [was] every day and Lombardi would put on *Howdy Doody* every single day. Lombardi put it on or would tell somebody to put it on. He'd have about six assistants there and they'd almost knock each other over to change the channel for him. We'd have a couple drinks before dinner. Tom Miller was there, of course, as the PR guy. He'd have a drink and do what Lombardi wanted. Vince Lombardi was a god, you know? The bar was in the back of the room and they'd have the lounge chairs in like a semicircle in front of the TV. It was not a football time, except when Lombardi wanted to know what was going on with the waiver wire or something like that. [Lombardi] would laugh, throw back his head and laugh if someone cracked a joke or at *Howdy Doody*.

[Lombardi and I] would pass each other on campus. Sure. The man was the man and he was his own man. And what he wanted he got. But I never bowed down to him and I think he respected that. And he knew that I respected him as a coach.

He ran those practice sessions on the practice field like Bear Bryant. Oh boy! He oversaw that entire situation. If those guys didn't get down and do those push-ups the right way, you could hear him all over Green Bay.

133

DAVE ANDERSON

Anderson was working for the New York Journal-American in 1964 when he agreed to write a story for Sport magazine and spent time at St. Norbert during training camp. A graduate of the College of the Holy Cross, Anderson began his newspaper career with the Brooklyn Eagle in 1951. He went to The New York Times in 1966 and became a columnist in 1971 when he joined the rotation that wrote Sports of the Times. He worked alongside Red Smith and Arthur Daley, although later he rotated with only Smith, and then others.

I went there in 1964 when Hornung was coming back from his suspension. In fact, I stayed at St. Norbert. I was following Hornung around. It was a piece for Sport magazine on Hornung coming back.

(Hornung had been suspended by Commissioner Pete Rozelle for gambling and sat out the 1963 season.)

After the afternoon practice one day and before dinner, the players had to get back to have dinner together at 6 o'clock at St. Norbert. It was a college cafeteria. You take a tray, get in line, get your food and sit down. I was with Hornung and he was ready to go, but Max McGee wasn't. I don't know what McGee was doing, whether he was in the whirlpool, getting treated for an injury or what. But he was just slow getting ready. And they were the last two to leave the locker room at Lambeau Field [then named City Stadium].

We get back [to St. Norbert], get in line for our food and everybody else is in there having dinner. They were the last two players and it was all right for me to be with them. They got their food; I got my food and we walked into the dining room and sat down in like the third or fourth row of tables. As we sat down, I could see Lombardi get up. He was in the front row and you could see him coming down the aisle. I'm saying, "Oh boy, he's coming after Hornung." He was coming after both of them actually and he came around and stood behind the two of them. There was a big clock on the wall and he pointed to the clock and said, "You're supposed to be here at 6 o'clock, not 10 after." They both kind of put their heads down and said, "Yes, coach." But you could probably hear it a mile away when [Lombardi] would bellow.

Now, it's the next day. It's after the morning practice and they're supposed to go back for lunch. Again, McGee is dawdling. Hornung says to him, "Max, Max, let's not be late for lunch." And they weren't. We just made lunch.

This was '64. Maybe I had a car and drove them. I know I had a car there. This was early in training camp. I had known Lombardi and was working for the Journal-American at the time in New York. I had gotten to know Lombardi when he was an assistant coach with the Giants. And, as you know, if you were from New York and he knew you, you could virtually get whatever you wanted. Plus, access was simple in those days.

[Lombardi] let me stay in Sensenbrenner Hall. The Giants did the same thing. That was normal procedure. Writers could stay in the dorms if they had to stay overnight.

LOU VOLPICELLI

Volpicelli produced and directed the television documentary Run to Daylight. *It was produced in 1964 and much of it was filmed on the St. Norbert campus. Volpicelli worked for ABC from 1952 until the mid-1980s. He received an Emmy for outstanding achievement in sports programming for his work on the 1968 Olympics and he was director of the acclaimed television series* Wide World of Sports *from 1960 to 1985. Volpicelli graduated from the University of Scranton in 1948. He currently lives in Darien, Conn.*

It was one of the most memorable assignments I've ever had in my professional life. When I was initially introduced to Mr. Lombardi, I immediately realized this man potentially would be immortalized in the name of sports. He could have been a member of the cloth at any time he would have so desired. I was very much impressed to see him every morning serve Mass and deliver Holy Communion and so on.

[*Run to Daylight*] was written by one of the great sportswriters, Bill

Heinz. My wife is in New York and she calls. She says, "Lou, you have a call from Howard Cosell." I answer at his command and he says *(at that point, Volpicelli began to imitate Cosell's nasal accent as he said),* "Volapecilli, I want you to come to my home in Pound Ridge and you're going to be my director for *Run to Daylight.*" So I go up to the meeting. The date was set and then we were off to Green Bay. There was myself, a cameraman, an audio man and, obviously, Howard. It was a little town and I think there was a bar wherever I looked.

I thought [St. Norbert] was fantastic and we were treated royally. When I meet or see people, I'm my own Central Casting type guy. The first thing I'd cast Mr. Lombardi as was one of those wonderful priests. Have you ever gone to the Vatican? Remember some of these wonderful priests that you'd see with a hat? [Lombardi] would be perfect for Central Casting.

Geez, how do I express this [about my first meeting with Lombardi]? What is this bullshit? Everybody thinks this guy is a tyrant. This is one of the most gentle human beings I've ever met in my life. He was almost like a saint and I mean that sincerely.

I think I helped tell that story with Howard Cosell by having my camera on top of the church steeple. That was the way the show opened. It was a wide-angle shot of the campus and three images appear on the screen: Two nuns walking toward the church and Mr. Lombardi. He walked to them and the conversation was as simple as this: "Good morning, Mr. Lombardi." "Good morning, sisters." From that extreme close-up, I took a close-up of his face. And as he turned around, I dissolved to him [doing] what he did best; in essence, the lines were something to the effect, "I want you to run, run, run to daylight." Then you see Hornung and the team run to daylight.

(Volpicelli said he couldn't be sure if he was filming from a church steeple or Main Hall.)

Mr. Cosell was a little askance [at St. Norbert] about even approaching this man, who was almost sacrosanct. I found out Mr. Lombardi enjoyed playing gin. And Howard Cosell—God bless him!—was one of the best gin players I ever met. I said [to Cosell], "Why don't you challenge him to a gin game?" From then on, the rapport between the two gentlemen was sensational. The last day of the shoot was when we literally talked to everybody and captured it on film. Then and only then did Howard Cosell, as I recall, under a beautiful tree, get his typical, beautifully done, in-depth interview with Mr. Lombardi.

If there was any irritation [between Cosell and Lombardi], it wasn't something I was privy to. I would say—if God willing, all of us go to heaven—I think Mr. Lombardi's quote would be, "Howard Cosell is a professional."

I was there for an entire month. The rumors were that [Lombardi] didn't do much as far as publicity events. But after I finished the film, Vince Lombardi came to New York to watch the playing of the documentary, probably through the persuasive qualities of Cosell. I'm not sure if it was the "21" Club or Toots Shor's. When it ended, there was a standing ovation for the documentary and it motivated Mr. Lombardi to go to the podium. The honor I had was when he mentioned what a pleasure it was to work with Lou Volpicelli.

(Lombardi traveled to New York on Sept. 3, 1964, to watch the preview of the show. He rejoined the Packers the next day in Cleveland where they closed the preseason against the Browns on Sept. 5.)

[Lombardi] was the most cordial guy. He allowed me to bring my cameras in when he gave his talk to the entire team. I remember it was around 7:15 at night. The scene was [him saying], "We want winners. We only want winners." My concentration was doing my job. We had only the one cameraman. [But] I felt privileged and honored that I was allowed to go into the room. I slept in the same dorms as these guys. I remember each one of these guys: [Jerry] Kramer, Hawg Hanner, Hornung obviously, Ray Nitschke, Jim Taylor, Willie Wood.

I remember at night the curfew was strictly held. Someone became the officer of the day. And there were some nights that the rounds were made by the master [Lombardi] himself. As a matter of fact, I remember one of the local priests ordered a pizza, which was delivered around 11 o'clock. As I recall, Mr. Lombardi approached with the thought that the person holding this pizza was one of the ballplayers.

Apologies followed because it was obvious that one of the priests had ordered it.

The service in the dining room was cafeteria style. The thing that captured my imagination was that Mr. Lombardi strategically placed himself at the end of where the food was being served because that was where the ice cream and goodies were. It was my recollection that a lot of the players didn't take anything [because of that].

The grin that Mother Nature and God blessed [Lombardi] with, with those teeth, so much was told when he smiled. But the smiles you had to figure out yourself: what he was thinking about.

I remember when I was in the service during World War II. There was this major—and my first day as a private—he ordered the company to attention and then he said, "I want everybody to jump." We all jumped. Then the major said, "Who told you to come down?" And then we were all told to take 10 laps. Lombardi didn't do this, but whatever he asked [his players] to do, they did it not under duress, but because they absolutely loved that human being, Mr. Lombardi.

CHAPTER 7

⚜

Family, Friends and Others

VINCE LOMBARDI JR.

Lombardi was a junior in high school in the winter of 1959 and enrolled at the old Premontre High School after his father was named head coach of the Packers and the family moved to Green Bay. He played football there the following fall and then at St. Thomas College. He graduated from St. Thomas in 1964 and from the William Mitchell College of Law in 1969. Vince Jr. served as assistant general manager of the Seattle Seahawks, assistant executive director of the NFL Management Council, and president and general manager of both the Michigan and Oakland franchises in the former United States Football League before becoming a professional speaker.

I was a ball boy, water boy, the first four, five years my father was there. One year in high school and four years in college, I was there the whole time. When you're in college you don't pay much attention to that stuff, but the St. Norbert campus was very nice. Lot of trees, grass. It was very conducive to the whole training camp environment, I think. I never heard guys complain about the surroundings per se, anyway.

I stayed at the dorm and there was an office right inside the door. I was right there, almost adjacent to the office, as I recall. The neat thing was that my mother thought I was at training camp, and my dad oftentimes thought I was at home. And a lot of times I was neither. One time I had been out all night and in the afternoon, I kind of lay down to take a little snooze behind a couple tackling dummies. My father saw something and said, "Who the hell is that?" The guys got a chuckle out of that.

[My dad] stayed [at St. Norbert] periodically. A lot of times he went home. He stayed over by the priests, I think. It could have been another dorm. I know he didn't go home all the time. He might have been in a different building.

I had [gone to training camp] the entire time my dad was with the Giants. I did for high school, college: Eight, nine years. So it wasn't a big, big deal. But guys became friends. When we first went to Green Bay, players were a little suspicious of me. When I was with the Giants, I was an assistant coach's kid, so what? But when I got there I was the head coach's kid. But Emlen Tunnell was there and he pretty quickly told them there was nothing to worry about, that I wasn't going to tell any tales. In fact, every time I might have mentioned something to my father, he'd go, "Don't tell me that. I don't want to know." So it wasn't a big deal. Let's put it this way, it beat the other jobs he'd find for me. He'd find me the crappiest jobs and about the middle of summer he'd say, "You want to go to training camp." "Hell, yes, I want to go to training camp." Yeah, I'd be working construction or at the Green Bay pickle factory or something. I played ball in high school and college, so it was good for me to be there and work out.

I ate [on campus]. When I got a little older, you could drink at 18 in those days, so a couple times my dad would have me take a guy to a tavern to get him a couple of beers before dinner because they wanted to put some weight on him. They were guys who didn't stick. I had all kinds of duties. I'd even hang out with some of those guys after I got old enough. Their attitude was: "If young Vince is with us, how much trouble can we get in?" Some of them became pretty good friends. I'd go over to Buck's. Early on that didn't happen. But the last couple years when I was old enough, I'd run into those guys. I'd run into them downtown when they had a night off.

They were all favorites. Jerry Kramer, I got to be pretty good buddies with him. Bart [Starr]. Gary Knafelc was always worth a laugh. Some guys would just take more of an interest in you as a person than others. Willie Davis. Some guys would be nice to you just to be nice. Fuzzy [Thurston]. Jim Ringo. Bob Skoronski. [Forrest] Gregg. They were all good guys. There was no water on the [practice] field. But there would be ice buckets for injuries. So the ice would melt and I'd periodically take a towel and soak it in the ice bucket, take it in the huddle and guys would grab it and suck on it.

A lot of times my dad would be sitting in that office at night. He certainly had a presence when [the players] would check in initially. I'd go there and eat, and then I'd take off unless it was my job to sit in the office and answer the phone, which was probably a couple days during the week. I'd see [my dad] walk across campus a lot to and from dinner.

They had that 5 o'clock club every night and they'd have a couple pops and let their hair down a little. But my dad didn't know that word relax. He'd have a couple Scotches on a Friday or Saturday or Sunday during the season. But he was pretty much always on edge, especially during training camp when he had a lot of work to do.

He had a whole gaggle of New York buddies. Mike Manuche was a good friend of my dad's and he owned a restaurant in New York. He would come out. And his son at one time was a ball boy, a couple years after I left. But, yeah, he'd have a lot of guys come in, maybe not so much during training camp as during the season. Eddie Breslin, whose sister was married to Art Modell. Manuche had this great restaurant in New York. Manuche's was a place that if you were in New York and wanted to see what sports personalities from out of town were in town, it was either Manuche's or Toots Shor's. The Giants used to go in Manuche's quite a bit.

If nothing else, [being at St. Norbert] made [my dad's] life a lot easier in terms of going to church and that kind of stuff. He was always comfortable around priests. He enjoyed their company. He grew up with them. We always had priests in our house. That wasn't the end all and be all, but it certainly helped. The other thing was that the nuns were always walking around campus and he loved chatting with them. "Hello sister, how are you?" That sort of thing. They were there for summer school. They used to get a kick out of that. It was very friendly. [My dad] wasn't in awe of them or anything. He just respected their vocation and their calling.

My mother would come to just about every [practice] session in the afternoon. I don't recall her being at St. Norbert other than at team functions like after a preseason game.

I don't know that I have any stories [about players sneaking out after curfew] other than they'd be giggling about it the next day. Everybody knows that history [about Max McGee]. He was a free spirit. He heard a different drummer than a lot of them. My dad wasn't a Boy Scout for crying out loud. As long as it didn't affect his play and his preparation and his effort, it wasn't the end of the world.

Hell and damn. Jesus, Mary and Joseph kind of thing. "What the hell is going on?" But, no, my dad didn't use the f-word. He was a bright guy. He could express himself without using those words. He was tough on [the players] all the time, particularly if the films didn't look good or they weren't picking things up. He was very demanding. You had to break them down to build them up. That was his attitude. I didn't go to meetings, but I heard him growl. Maybe he didn't like how they were dressed on campus with all those nuns or something like that. I don't recall any real outbursts, at least not on campus.

Dad Braisher worked so hard, putting in so many hours. Plus, he lived right there in De Pere. I don't remember him being on campus all that much. I can recall a lot of times going back from lunch and bringing him his lunch from the dining room. I don't think either of those guys [Braisher or Bud Jorgensen] were on the campus. They lived in town.

(G.E. "Dad" Braisher was equipment manager of the Packers from 1956 to 1976. Jorgensen, who worked for the Packers from 1924 to 1971, was the team trainer during the Lombardi era.)

The [players would] get up. They'd have breakfast. Get on the bus, go out and practice. Come back. Eat, take a little nap, go back out. Come back again, take a little nap, go eat. Go to meetings, go to bed.

SUE LOMBARDI

Sue was 12 years old when her family moved to Green Bay in 1959. Seven years later, she graduated from the old St. Joseph Academy. She currently lives in the Jacksonville, Fla., area with her husband, James Taylor.

My brother was [at St. Norbert] a lot. He stayed in the dorms and all that. The only thing I did—my mother and I—was go to every practice. As far as going over to St. Norbert, I didn't get to the campus at all. It was just understood that it wasn't a place for me. [My father] was strict and he had his standards as far as what he believed about women. Not that he was a sexist, by any means. He believed in equal rights and all that. But when it came to football and me being a girl and his princess, princesses just don't go to football camps.

In the beginning years, [my father] never came home. He stayed at [St. Norbert]. He literally went to camp and that was it. When he was with the Giants, he went to Oregon. So it was nothing for me not to have my father home during training camp. Later years [at St. Norbert], [my father] came home at night. But it wasn't early night; it was late night. And I was getting to the age where I wasn't home, either.

When training camp rolled around, I was never so happy to see a man leave the house in my entire life. *(She let out a hearty laugh.)* It was tough. He started to get antsy. You could just feel the tension starting, that he was anxious.

JACK KOEPPLER

Koeppler, a Green Bay insurance agent, was one of Lombardi's friends and golfing partners. He also served on the Packers' board of directors for 34 years until he died at age 82 in May 2009. He was interviewed for this book five months before his death.

We'd sit around and bullshit for maybe 45 minutes [at the 5 o'clock club]. Lombardi drank Scotch. Jake Stathas was always

143

out there. Tony Canadeo was usually there. We talked mostly golf because that was during the season of golf. Lombardi played every Saturday. When Green Bay was at home, he marched the team through kickoff and punt returns. And at 12 o'clock, we teed off. If Green Bay was playing Chicago at home, on Saturday afternoon, he played golf. I'm not sure about training camp, but I think he did on Saturday afternoons [if the Packers weren't practicing].

(Canadeo, one of the Packers' all-time greats and a 1974 inductee into the Pro Football Hall of Fame, was one of Lombardi's close friends and also a member of the Packers' executive committee at the time. Stathas was another one of Lombardi's good friends and a member of the Packers board of directors.]

The funniest thing that ever happened out there was [one year] at the first meal of camp—nobody started to eat until Lombardi sat down—Lombardi was walking through and goes by Elijah Pitts. Lombardi was about three steps past him when he came to an abrupt halt. He said, "Elijah what the hell is that?" Elijah had a goatee. Elijah says, "Coach, it's a goatee." Lombardi said, "Go get rid of the goatee before you eat because you're not eating with it."

PAT COCHRAN

Pat is the widow of John "Red" Cochran, who was a member of Lombardi's original coaching staff in Green Bay. Pat and Red were married in 1956. Red died at age 82 in 2004 after spending 42 years with the Packers as a coach and scout. He was on Lombardi's staff from 1959 to 1966. Pat lives in West De Pere.

Vince allowed the boy children of the coaches to come and have dinner with them and spend a night at Sensenbrenner Hall. That was kind of a fun thing. I took my son out there and I was waiting for Red to come and pick him up. We were sitting inside the dining hall. Here comes Vince, "Ah, Russell." He opens the door and grabs the kid and asks, "Where's his suitcase?" Now, Russell wouldn't even eat a hot dog he was such a picky eater. I thought, "Oh gosh, isn't this going to be fun?" But the kid's eyes were big as saucers. Russell was about 5 or 6. He wasn't very old. But Vince started talking to him and off they went. Red comes along and I said, "You won't believe it. Vince has him in the dining room." You know Vince; you never knew what to expect from him.

Red ate over there, slept over there. Once in awhile, he'd come home and sometimes have a cocktail with me. The joke was to bring his dirty clothes home and he'd pop in. The early years we lived in Allouez, but [Red] always stayed there [at St. Norbert].

Those guys, when training camp came, they got the urge. Let me tell you, Red Cochran, at training camp time when he was 80 years old, you couldn't talk to him. They never get over that. You can pick away at 'em and talk to 'em and they're not with you because it's training camp. They all spent their lives in football.

The women, the time we could go out there was when [Lombardi] had these nice dinners after the home preseason games. Shrimp by the mountains. Really good food. It was nice and the guys could get loose. They still had a time they had to be in, but [Lombardi] was a little looser with them after those games and they could go out and play a little. The mood depended on whether you won or lost. But you didn't lose with Lombardi. He thought if you didn't win those preseason games, you weren't going to win during the season. "Winning becomes a habit." I can hear that yet.

Sometimes Vince could be almost fun. We used to call him, "The Happy Italian." He wasn't very happy very often, but for those family things, he was like "The Godfather." And Marie was such a good person. A lot of people were afraid of her, but you just had to get to know her a little bit. She took care of us women. Vince could do nothing without Marie. They fought like cats and dogs, but I'll tell you, if she wasn't around at any social thing, he was lost.

I remember one time during training camp, I think [the players] had to midnight and we were downtown with Max and Paul [Hornung]. Red and I used to run with the ballplayers a little bit. I was their age. I use to feed them, have them over to the house. And we'd go out with them. We're sitting down there, probably at Wally's

Spot, down by Prange's; either that or Speed's. Red said, "Now, damn it, go home. You've got 15 minutes, get out of here and go back to the dorm." Of course, they didn't. I remember Max would say, "Gull darn, Red. We bought you drinks all night and then you turn us in." I loved Max. He was too much.

(The Spot Supper Club was located at 425 N. Washington St. in downtown Green Bay.)

JOHN GORDON

Gordon assisted "Dad" Braisher in the equipment room during training camp in the 1960s. A native of Green Bay, Gordon graduated from St. Norbert College in 1964. He worked for the Packers while he was a student, as well as after graduation. He also is still affiliated with the college, serving as an adjunct assistant professor of art.

I roomed right there in the same dorm as the players. I think it was from '61 through '67. One year, I worked the whole season. I think that was 1962. I worked with Dad and I also helped out Bud Jorgensen. I taped ankles and that sort of thing.

I'd put the jocks and socks and the T-shirt—making rolls—in each locker. I'd bring the equipment down to the practice field and set up things, whatever they needed me to do. [I'd go to St. Norbert] just to sleep and to eat. We'd leave St. Norbert and go to practice. I'd come back after the team left [the stadium] in the evening. I didn't spend a lot of time there except in the evening.

I remember the players sometimes would just sit outside on the steps there at Sensenbrenner and the little kids in the neighborhood would come around. I have one memory and it's very strong. Remember Ben Davidson? He was one of the sweetest guys and he'd tell the kids how he used to get his pants cuff caught in the chain of his bike and all that. He was talking just to the kids and they really liked him. Huge. They [traded] him.

(Davidson, a 6-8, 275-pound defensive end, played for the Packers in 1961. He was traded to Washington before the 1962 season. He later

played eight years with the Oakland Raiders and faced the Packers in Super Bowl II.)

[Lombardi] would go to Mass every morning and I'd see him do that. [Otherwise], I didn't see much of him. I just tried to avoid him. Just his presence. He'd forget my name every year. He was a powerful guy. I still am [afraid of him]. I still hear his voice when I screw up. He was so commanding and he wasn't always attentive to where he was. Deep in thought often when he was alone.

It was quite an experience [living in the dorm with the Packers], but it became normal after I was there for so long. Mostly the rookies were friendliest to me. So I got to know them very well, particularly Elijah Pitts, who let me use his car over the summer. It had no battery, so it basically sat next to my house. But we could jump it to get it going.

I remember an incident on the practice field involving Max McGee and it culminated in the cafeteria at St. Norbert. Anyway, he called me over [on the practice field] and said, "You see those two girls over there." So he pointed out the two girls and said, "Go tell them I'll meet them at Jimmie's Bamboo Room at 10 o'clock." So I ran over there—I thought he knew them—and gave them the message. The girl said, "Who is Max McGee?" I pointed him out and that was it. The next morning, I'm having breakfast and there are only a few players around. Lombardi is there and McGee walks in. Lombardi says, "McGee, that will be $1,000." McGee said, "That's a lot of money, coach." Lombardi said, "Pay it or get out." That was the last I heard of that.

(Jimmie's Bamboo Room was located at 3754 Riverside Dr., across the street from Minahan Stadium.)

Being cut, that was difficult. I remember playing pool down in Sensenbrenner. The guys were playing pool and one of the [rookies] I really liked was named Green as I recall. Word came that he had got cut. He was going to leave in the morning and he said, "Well, I'll come back and visit you guys." Willie Wood said, "You don't want to do that." Or something. It was very strong, like "Don't even try that." He had made friends and stuff, and the old veterans just said, "Unh—unh."

DOUG BROZEK

Brozek grew up in De Pere and had a tryout with the Packers in 1963. After graduating from De Pere High School in 1959, Brozek started playing semi-pro football for the Manitowoc Chiefs the following fall. He remained with the Chiefs for close to 15 years, playing defensive tackle and also doubling as coach for most of that period.

What happened was, I called [the Packers] and then they sent down to Manitowoc for some film. They called me the next day and I went to like a mini-camp and worked out for like three days with Forrest Gregg. Then they signed me to a contract. Back then there was no money. My contract was 7,500 bucks. Guys like Fuzzy were making maybe $30,000.

I remember one night [at St. Norbert] a bunch of us guys ordered a bunch of pizzas. I don't know if they thought we were having a party or what, but one of the assistant coaches came up and told us to calm down a little bit. Evidently, we were making too much noise, having too much fun. Marv Fleming was there. Lionel Aldridge. They were rookies also. We were on the second floor and there were two people to each room. Back then we didn't have the money to go out or anything. We were just laughing, telling jokes, telling stories.

I can't remember anybody saying anything bad about [Lombardi] at all in the dorms. He was a different breed. He demanded respect and he got it. You used to see him coming from church every morning. We'd be going to breakfast and he'd be coming from Mass.

I had access to a car and so I was like the chauffeur. We'd go down to Green Bay if we had a night off and didn't have to go to films. We'd go down to like Speed's, the Piccadilly. [Lombardi] never said anything to us during training camp about those places being off limits. I hung out mostly with rookies. When you traveled from the college to the field, you went on school buses. Ninety percent of the guys didn't have a car. I don't think any of the rookies did.

(The Piccadilly Club was located at 242 Main Blvd. in Green Bay, close to where a McDonald's Restaurant stands. The Piccadilly was

notorious for being the Packers' hangout when they were losing badly in the 1950s.)

I sang with Lionel. We made it up. We sang *Hey Laddy Laddy Lo.* "I know a guy whose name is Starr. He's a guy you wouldn't find in a bar. I know a guy named Ringo, he's a guy who plays bingo." [We] got a lot of laughs.

We used to ask the bus driver [following the afternoon practice] to stop the bus [in West De Pere], so we could go in and pick up a paper. That was at Stowe's Drug Store. We'd pick up a paper, leave, walk down the street and go into the Dehn's Ice Cream place. We'd go in there in case anybody saw us, go out the backdoor and go next door to a bar. They had like a little building in between with a garden, and we'd go sit in that garden and buy quarts of beer. We'd have maybe an hour before dinner was served. We had to jog back so we made it in on time for dinner. Lombardi had told us we weren't supposed to be going into taverns.

(Dehn's was at 330 Main Ave. in West De Pere, where Luna Coffee is currently located.)

Remember Buck's? It was over on Fourth and Reid streets. There was a guy everybody would buy beers for because he could chug like a 12-ounce bottle straight down. I think he was a big defensive lineman. We used to sit in the booths. Even the veterans would buy them for him and watch him. But I remember only a couple of times going to Buck's.

[When I got cut] somebody knocked on the door and said, "Mr. Lombardi would like to see you in his office." That was it. [Lombardi] had an office right on campus. I believe in Sensenbrenner. He said, "You're a good football player, but you're trying out for the world championship team. So we're going to have to let you go, but I'll give you a recommendation to any team looking for a defensive lineman." That was about it. You pack your bags and find yourself a way home. Some of the guys had already gone back out to the practice field. You might see your roommate. I knew I was a long shot. I think I realize now more than before how close I was and how much it would have meant to me. [Lombardi] was very professional. We shook hands and it was over.

A Championship Team

AL GROVES

After playing football at St. Norbert, Groves was drafted by the Packers as a defensive tackle in the 16th round of the 1968 NFL draft. His tryout was brief, but he later spent 24 years coaching at the old De Pere Abbot Pennings High School, eight of those as head coach. The 2010 football season will be Groves' 12th as an assistant coach at St. Norbert.

When Fr. Burke was there, I was staying up in the summer for different things and I was an altar server. Fr. Burke was saying Mass and Lombardi was at Mass. For one, even though I'm 6-4, I remember feeling small; Lombardi wasn't necessarily that tall, but because of his stature and Fr. Burke was a big guy and a very important person. And, obviously, Lombardi was an important person. I was probably in awe at the time.

That was previous to my being drafted. I guess I was probably a junior at the time. I was from Milwaukee originally. [I'd stay in the summer] to work and work out with Howie [Kolstad]. I didn't stay on campus. I don't remember seeing the Packers much other than when I was drafted and tried out.

(Kolstad was the St. Norbert football coach from 1960 to 1978.)

You'd see [the Packers] walking like we do now. There was probably an overlap of a week or two with our training camp and theirs, [but] they stayed in a different dorm than we did. I remember them being in Sensenbrenner; and I have a feeling we were in Burke, which was Berne back then. You'd see them walking the sidewalks and that was about it. I don't remember ever talking to anybody when I was playing at St. Norbert and when I was drafted, I was only there for a few days.

JIM HUGHES

Hughes lived virtually across the street from Sensenbrenner Hall and spent his summers as a youngster hanging around the Packers on the St. Norbert campus. Hughes' family lived at 131 Marsh St. in a house

150

that was torn down to make way for the Schuldes Sports Center, which opened in 1979. The family's yard extended from roughly the backend of Schuldes to the Fox River. James Hughes, his late father, played football for and graduated from St. Norbert in the 1930s. Jim graduated from Pennings in 1974 and from the University of Wisconsin-La Crosse in 1979. He is living in Wauwatosa and is a part owner of a craft beer business.

We grew up on the end of Marsh Street, the last house before the river. I would say from Sensenbrenner Hall, we were 200 yards. So in the summer of '62, I was starting to become pretty aware of the Packers. And the first time I ever went over to St. Norbert, I met Bart Starr. I was hanging around and I got his autograph or something. The next day, I broke my leg. I jumped off my neighbor's porch, which I probably had jumped off 100 times. I broke my leg in four places and one of the neighbor kids told Starr, "Jimmy Hughes, who lives over there, broke his leg." I had a cast up to my waist and Starr came over about a week later. I was on the couch; I was in a wheelchair. That's how I moved around. My sister answered the door and there was Bart Starr. It kind of blew her away. He came over three times and I think the second time he came with a football signed by half of the '62 Packers, the famous 13-1 Packers. He encouraged me to get up, get better and go get the football signed by the other half, which I did. The third time, he came with a junior Packer uniform for me. From that time on, Starr and I had a really good relationship. He was great to me. I was going to be in first grade. I was six years old. So that was the first year I really got to know them all and I was hanging around all the time.

The worst part of the story is I lost [the football] in the river. I played with it. I lost it in the river, like I probably lost one hundred balls in the river.

But that started all my connection with the Packers. I had lunch at the Union with them. Starr just brought me over. He'd have the assistant coaches bring me out to practice. I probably went to two or three practices once I was on crutches. He'd have like Norb Hecker or Tom

Fears drive me out to practice. There were always two school buses that took the team to practice. I wouldn't be on the field. I'd hang in the bleachers and wait for practice to get over and ride back with the assistant coaches.

I remember Starr had a Ford Thunderbird and he said, "Come on, Jimmy, we're going to go over to Derrick's A&W and get you an ice cream." He would give money to kids. The kids would all be sitting out there [on campus] and Starr would give everybody a quarter. He'd go, "Why don't you guys all go get an ice cream?" He'd give out three dollars worth of quarters to the kids who would be hanging out there. He was so nice to the kids. I remember vividly jumping in Starr's Thunderbird with Gary Knafelc and I was in the backseat, and they brought me to the A&W.

So I was probably closer to Starr than any of the Packers, but because of that I became very comfortable just hanging around. And it was so close, so for my summers, I would wait for the players to come to check in and I would help all the players check in with their luggage. Some would tip me; some wouldn't. But I wouldn't go there to make money. It was fun for me. They'd pull up in their cars. I remember Elijah Pitts pulling up in this old jalopy of a car. By '64, '65, they all knew me by name.

Lombardi knew me real well and I've got a couple Lombardi stories at St. Norbert. The Packers would have their offensive and defensive meetings in the basement of Sensenbrenner Hall and I can remember many, many times watching Lombardi conduct meetings—it was always the offense—through the window. I'd just kind of peer in through the blinds. Lombardi knew it was me. He didn't chase me out of there.

I got to know him so well that in '66, he had the son of the New York Giants' attorney who was a good friend of his—his name was O'Hara—come out to work for the Packers and stay in the dorm. The son's name was J.P. O'Hara. Lombardi, like the day before J.P. came out, said, "Jimmy, I've got a great New York friend who is sending his son out for the summer and I want to make sure he's having fun. He's going to be working for the Packers." So I got to know J.P. really well.

(The father's name was William J. Pat O'Hara. Not only a friend, Pat O'Hara also was one of Lombardi's classmates at Fordham University.)

The next year, [Lombardi] did it again. That year it was a kid named Mike Manuche. If you go back to *When Pride Still Mattered,* there were a lot of references to Lombardi spending time in an Italian restaurant named Manuche's. Lombardi asked me again—this was '67—and I got to know Mike real well. He went up to our cottage for a weekend. Lombardi let him go. I'd just hang around in Manuche's dorm room. He was my age. I was 12 in '67. Lombardi didn't want the kid to be bored. He knew my parents a little bit, so he was comfortable doing that. I remember sitting in a dorm room. It was Manuche and me, Jim Grabowski, Donny Anderson and Gale Gillingham. We were all watching *Mission Impossible.* I lived in that dorm by the time I was 12 and was there all the time.

Some of the players brought in portables [TVs]. I carried a few in for them. By '67, most of the guys had portable TVs. That wasn't true in '62.

My favorite Lombardi story was Bill Curry's rookie year. I think it was '65. His dorm room faced our house and we had a beagle. I'd be there at lunch. I'd be there at dinner. I'd just be hanging around. It was just cool to see the Packers. Curry said, "You that little boy that lives over there with that beagle?" I said, "Yeah, I am." He said, "Boy, I had a dog like that. Could you bring that dog over here?" I said, "Sure." I'm sitting outside Sensenbrenner Hall and Lombardi comes storming out. It must have been before dinner. He says, "Jimmy, get that goddamn dog out of here. This is a football training camp." He just lays into me. He did say, "Goddamn." I'm maybe 10 years old and I go home and tell my dad. My dad's reaction was like all of our parents at that time, "Well, I guess you shouldn't have had the dog there." I don't know how many days afterward that it was, but I was hanging out there again. Lombardi comes out and I'm being a little shy about it. Lombardi comes up to me and goes, "Hey Jimmy, where's that cute little dog of yours?" So when I'd hear and read about the hot-and-cold, volatile personality of Lombardi, I saw it. I caught the wrath of it.

You knew there were times to get out of his way. I got to understand his moods a little bit and he was always very nice to me except for that time. I saw him lose his patience with kids sometimes. I knew to call him "Coach" or "Mr. Lombardi." I'd see kids who'd show up once a summer. Their parents might say, "Hey, you want to get some autographs?" That used to happen every once in awhile and they'd maybe say, "Hey, Vince." He didn't like that when young kids called him Vince. I'm sure my dad was emphatic about that, too. Either call him "Coach Lombardi" or "Mr. Lombardi."

I remember Lombardi's room. He had a corner suite in Sensenbrenner Hall. It was a larger room in 1960s dorm vernacular. I could walk to the top of the steps, take a right and still go to that room. It would have been in the northwest corner of the first floor? Now, was he there all the time? I don't know that.

There would be days where six or seven [kids would be hanging out on the campus]. There would be days where maybe 10. I guess if anybody was consistently there every day, it was me, and that was strictly because of proximity. And one of the things I tell people that exemplifies what a different time it was: There were no security people around. You could walk right with [the Packers] from the time they left Sensenbrenner Hall until they got to the Union to eat. That was the typical place where kids would meet them. [The Packers] would come back from morning practice on the bus, maybe go into Sensenbrenner Hall and then walk over to lunch. They'd mosey past Ed Longteau's house on Second Street—and it was still Second Street then not [part of the] mall. And I remember how accommodating the players were about giving autographs and things like that. Then kids would wait for them outside the Union after lunch.

Once I got past the stage of getting autographs, maybe '64, it was no big deal. I remember Lombardi saying to me, "Jimmy, how many of my autographs do you have?" And he kind of laughed. I stopped asking for autographs and would just sit and talk with them.

Just to show you how naïve you could be growing up in West De Pere—and I'll never forget this and I've talked to Willie Davis about it. I remember walking from the Union down Second Street with Davis. They used to come out with handfuls of fruit: plums, apples, oranges. Davis gave me a plum. I'm embarrassed about this to this day, but I asked him, "How come the inside of your hands are white?" I had never been around a black guy before. I was at a meeting with Willie Davis one time and I told him that story and told him how nice he was to me. How, [he had said], "That's how God created me." I was maybe 8 years old.

A lot of times I'd be sitting next to Ed Longteau. Ed was our neighbor and such a friend to me. [The Packers] would always stop and talk to Ed. He was in his late 80s, 90s. Ed knew our whole family and was like a grandpa to me. I remember, Ed would say to me, "Look at the size of that guy." It was probably no different for Ed than the joy I got out of it. You knew these guys were world champions, the best football team in the land. They were legends. It was a cool thing.

My sisters always swore they'd see Hornung and McGee running in right around 11 o'clock, but I never saw that.

One of the more bizarre things I ever saw was Bob Brown—there was a line at the door to get in the St. Norbert Union—fainting like a box of rocks. I thought the guy died right in front of me. I'll never forget that: big Bob Brown just going down. He just keeled right over from two-a-days. It probably was a warm summer day. Those guys didn't come in shape; they came to get in shape.

There are so many memories. So many of these guys wore flip-flops. They all had their ankles shaved at that time. They'd be moving so slow. You could just tell they were hurting. The only guy I ever remember always moving around fast was Jimmy Taylor. He didn't want to spend any time with the kids. He'd have a cigar hanging out of his mouth sometimes and he was always moving fast.

It must have been 1963. They had their physicals over at Van Dyke Gym and I was hanging around Bart like I always did. I don't remember what players were there, but there was a whole group. They were starting with kind of a raunchy story and as soon as the story started, I remember Bart kind of grabbing me and saying, "Jimmy, I don't think you want to hear this." He pulled me away from the whole group of guys.

Sensenbrenner was kind of an L-shaped building and there was a little chapel in the southwest [corner of the basement]. My family used to go to Mass there if we didn't want to go over to St. Joseph. I remember on Sundays, I'd serve in this little chapel and one time I remember I served and it was Mrs. Van Gemert—the Van Gemerts lived on the corner of Second and Marsh streets—and Lombardi. That was it.

Henry Jordan was great to me. Herb Adderley was wonderful to me. So was Elijah Pitts. He was one of the nicest guys that I ever met. They'd sit and talk to you. I used to throw the ball around with Adderley in the little courtyard on the south side of Sensenbrenner. I'd so often have a football in my hand and Adderley would go, "Jimmy, go out for a pass." He would really spend time with me and ask, "How was your school year? What are you doing now?" All that type of stuff.

I was a little older, maybe 10 years old, and there was a knock on my door. I think it was a weekend, but during training camp. It was Marv Fleming. He says, "Hey, Jimmy." He goes, "My family is visiting from home and I know this is your yard, and I was wondering if we could have a picnic in your yard." Our yard was flat and [then] went down to the river. My parents weren't home, but I said, "Sure." About an hour later, my dad pulls in with my mom and there are like eight black people having a picnic in our front yard. Dad goes, "What's going on?" I said, "That's Marv Fleming. They wanted to have a picnic there and I thought it would be OK." My dad was an enlightened New Deal Democrat. So he was all for civil rights and he didn't have any problem with it. But he was a little taken aback.

I got to be a heavier kid. That's something else that pops into my mind. I wasn't a big fat slob, but I was like a lot of 10-, 11-year olds who hadn't stretched out yet. Forrest Gregg used to call me "Heavy Lunch" in that old southern drawl or Texas accent of his. "Hey, Heavy Lunch, you're getting kind of big this summer." I was eating a piece of Turkish taffy one time and there was like a bicycle rack that was green and gold—the St. Norbert colors—on Second Street. I was just sitting there and Henry Jordan came out and said, "Jimmy, it looks like you've been eating poop all morning." They'd kid around with me.

That summer that Manuche was there, I rode out to the practices on the team bus at least a dozen times. They'd all be talking back and forth. They all knew who I was, so they were very accepting. I'd wait for them to come out of the locker room and walk down to practice with some of them. They were already doing that tradition with kids riding on the bikes and I felt like big stuff because they all knew me. "Hey, Jimmy, see you at practice."

They were all really nice guys. So many of the guys who were kind of unknown were so nice. Phil Vandersea was a really nice guy. Bill Curry was just the nicest guy. Jim Flanigan was a good guy. I remember Bob Jeter giving me $5 to go get him a thing of eyedrops one time. I jumped on my bike and went to Stowe's [Drug Store].

I remember Lombardi being around a lot the summer he was general manager. It's not like he was invisible.

I remember Bud Lea being around there all the time. Lee Remmel. I knew who those guys were. I can't confirm it, but I think Dick Schaap was around. I remember Chuck Johnson was around. I knew who Chuck Johnson was because my dad was a Democrat and we'd get The Milwaukee Journal at home every night.

I knew that campus like the back of my hand. I knew every in and out, every nook and cranny. That was my playground. It was still very pretty. The Norbertine influence—in terms of seeing Norbertines around—was a lot more prominent. There was a sidewalk that kind of bordered the campus and I so vividly remember the Norbertines in their white robes walking around in the evenings and the summer, sometimes by themselves reading the Gospel or some type of Scripture. I remember some of the priests.

I have a great Fr. Burke story. Fr. Burke was a huge influence in the neighborhood and he had a charisma as great as Lombardi's. He filled up a room. He was like 6-6 and we knew him very well. He actually said my father's funeral Mass. I remember vividly I was like 9, 10 and there was a knock on the door and there was Fr. Burke in his white robes. He goes, "Jimmy, is your dad home?" I go, "No, Father, he's not." [Burke] had an apartment over in [what is] now Burke Hall, then Berne Hall. He said, "I've got a couple guests over in my apartment and I know where your dad leaves his Scotch." He walks into the kitchen, goes to the liquor cabinet and grabs a bottle of Scotch. "Let your dad know I have that." That didn't have anything to do with [training camp]. But Fr. Burke was around a lot. I think Fr. Burke loved the fact that the Packers were there.

MIKE MANUCHE

Michael Joseph Manuche, the son of one of Lombardi's close New York friends, spent the summer of 1968 as an aide in the Packers' equipment room. Michael's father, George Joseph Mike Manuche, owned a popular New York restaurant from 1951 to 1982 that catered to prominent sports figures. The restaurant was known as Manuche's and was located on West 52nd Street in the heart of Manhattan. It was one of Lombardi's favorite haunts from the time he was an assistant coach with the New York Giants. Michael Joseph is a commercial airline pilot living in San Diego. He's a graduate of Columbia University and a former Marine pilot.

I was 11 years old. I spent the summer the year Vince Lombardi was the general manager and Phil Bengtson was the head coach.

When I was 11, the Packers had just played the '68 Super Bowl and [Lombardi] was in New York. I had grown up in Westchester County, New York. Vince and his wife Marie were over for dinner at our house. I happened to be sitting in the living room with them and I remember Dad was smiling like something was going on. Then Vince Lombardi looks at me and says, "How would you like to spend the summer with the Green Bay Packers?" Even though I was only 11, it took me about two seconds to say, "Sure." He says, "Well, you're going to have to work. You're going to be assistant equipment manager and you're not just going to be on vacation." I said, "When do we leave?" That's basically how it came about. And it certainly beat summer camp in Connecticut.

I stayed in one of the dormitories at St. Norbert College. I had my own room there in the same area as all the players. I was basically a ball boy. I worked for a guy named Dad Braisher. Great guy. My duties were the same as most of the older guys who were doing that. I'd put together all the shirts, the jocks, the socks and put them in the lockers. That was when they first started Gatorade and I put that together for the practices. I'd put facemasks on helmets, run balls around, bring out water or Gatorade to the players during breaks. I was kept pretty busy.

It was usually at Mass when I [saw Lombardi on campus]. He often wanted me to go and I'd go to Mass with him in the morning. Most of the time, I saw him at the practice facility. He'd go out there and watch. He did not want to interfere and perhaps I'm superimposing my dad's thoughts on some of my memories. But I think it was difficult for him. There was a big tower in the middle of the field and he would go up there and watch. I don't ever recall him shouting at players or doing any coaching.

My greatest memory was that all the players treated me like a team member and I was a rookie. So I had to sing like a rookie in front of all the players. I remember [Lombardi] was there for that. I got to do the same thing the next year at Carlisle, Pennsylvania, when [Lombardi] was coaching Washington. I don't actually remember what I sang in Green Bay. The song the players wrote for me in Carlisle was: "You're Nobody Until Lombardi Loves You."

At that point, the Packers had been under the influence of Lombardi for so long, even as an 11-year old kid, the class these guys had was really something. My last preseason game was against the Cowboys in Dallas. I had to go back to school and went around at dinner saying goodbye. I was so upset about leaving I was crying.

I was 11 and I had to be in bed at 10 o'clock. I remember Ray Nitschke coming in many nights at 10 o'clock when I was sound asleep in my room and going, "Hey, Mickie, you asleep?" Checking to make sure I was in bed. I remember being in a lounge room in the dormitory and going in there and watching TV with players at night.

I spent a lot of time with Marv Fleming. He taught me how to shoot a bow-and-arrow, believe it or not. Somewhere on the campus, we went over and he had a bow-and-arrow. So when I got home, I was intent on getting a bow-and-arrow for a birthday or Christmas. I grew up in pretty much a lily-white neighborhood and Marv

Fleming used to talk to me about being black and what it means. That was a bit of an education for a young man.

I was on campus one time and missed the bus to go to practice in the morning. There was something called, "Lombardi time," which was 15 minutes early. I actually made it to where the bus left five minutes before it was supposed to leave, but it was gone already. Now, I couldn't get to practice and I was a little bit panicking. Somewhere on campus there were some offices [for the Packers] and the gentleman in there—I think it was Chuck Lane—gave me a ride to practice. I get over there and Vince Lombardi was there. He fined me 25 cents for being late. I protested that I was there five minutes early and he said, "Well, now you know about Lombardi time." He fined me 25 cents and kept it, too.

I used to go fishing for carp in the river right there. I remember once or twice players being surprised that I caught these huge carp out of that river using little balled up pieces of bread. I was pretty busy. The fun part was being around the players all the time: not just being at practice, but being on the campus and living in the dormitory with them.

BILL BOHNE

Bohne has been teaching in the art department at St. Norbert College since 1965. A native of Youngstown, Ohio, he moved to the Green Bay area that year after getting a graduate degree at Ohio University.

I was introduced to [Lombardi] one day when I just happened to be on The Green walking across campus. I saw Fr. Burke and there was another person with him whom I didn't recognize from a distance. When I realized it was Coach Lombardi, he was a lot smaller than I thought he'd be. He had already established himself as a coach, this being 1965. I had just arrived in town. So Fr. Burke saw me and he said, "Coach Lombardi, I'd like to introduce you to one of our new faculty members." Lombardi gave that big, gap-toothed smile and extended his hand. We shook hands and he said to me—and I'll never forget this—"You know, you have the most important job—teaching, that is." That meant a lot to me. I knew already that as a coach, he was the consummate teacher himself. There were other pleasantries, small conversation and some remark about, "We need to get some good Italian restaurants in Green Bay."

[Fr. Burke] was about 6-foot-5. Have you ever seen the photograph of [Burke and Lombardi] standing in front of Sensenbrenner? That was in Time magazine. I don't remember the year; it was the late Sixties, early Seventies. What a sharp move that was from the stand-point of marketing and advertising. The picture, as they say, spoke one thousand words. It was in the Midwest edition. They were doing the regional things even then. I think there was some copy under-neath it about a partnership. It referred to the fact that these two guys had gotten together and the Packers had become part of St. Norbert.

As an artist, I'm a fairly astute observer. I would see that nuns would be on campus during the summer. It would overlap with train-ing camp and I'd see the Packers interacting with [them]. That was back when they were all in habits. There were theological studies here and they took other courses in education. Nowadays, they call them in-service training courses. I had a studio on campus and I'd work there, and be out and about. It was kind of comical seeing these big guys talking to the nuns. Sometimes I was close enough to hear little comments: "We're going to pray for you." "Thank you so much." [The players] were very accommodating with these sisters. And [the nuns] would go, "God bless you" when they'd leave. I would see [Lombardi] talk with them.

You know [Lombardi] was a very religious person and I think that colored a lot of things. After his death, I began to think about how out East he was pretty much connected to the Jesuits. For him to come here and become close to the Norbertines was another thing all together because they are very different religious orders. The Norbertines are very progressive and fairly liberal by comparison. You could say the strictness of the Jesuit education and training was something imparted to Lombardi—that and the military. Of course, he coached at West Point.

I remember the first time I saw Fr. Burke. He was an imposing figure. I went to his office and was introduced to him. This was part of the interview process. You had to meet with the dean, and then you went and met with the president. He [Burke] was a hands-on guy. It wasn't necessarily a control thing, but he wanted to be on top of it, so I spent maybe a half-hour with him in his office. He was behind his desk when I came in and he stood up. His desk, as I recall, was elevated a little bit and there was a beam of wood above his head that had recessed lights in it. He had a white robe on. So it was theatrical in many ways. He was a guy who really ran a tight ship. And Lombardi was pretty rigid that way, too, with the military training he had. It was almost classic East Coast with the Irish and Italians getting together. You had those kinds of alliances in the larger cities, particularly in Boston and New York. I think they knew their particular ethnic backgrounds; that the Irish and Italians had to struggle a lot when they came to this country. And the other common thing was their religion.

From the standpoint of aesthetics, it was [a beautiful] campus back then but it's even better now. As an artist, I didn't find it particularly exciting from the standpoint of architecture. I thought Main Hall was really a nice building, very representative of the period. But I wasn't nuts about [the rest]. There's more of a green flow or natural flow now with the walkways than there was then. Everything was defined by the street grids at that point. Once they got rid of the streets, things became more intimate. Former students come back now and they can't believe what has happened. It's a different place. [In the 1960s] town and gown kind of meshed together.

In 1965, Second Street was still there. That's where the mall is now. In 1965, the John Minahan Science Building was not there. There were old Victorian houses where that building is now. So on the corner of Second and Reid there were homes. Across the street was a funeral home, on the southwest corner of Reid and Second. Grant Street went directly through the campus, all the way to the river. It went right in front of Boyle Hall and the old St. Joe's parochial school. It was a neighborhood. There were old homes, many of them built in the late 19th century, along Second Street. Abbot Pennings eventually owned a lot of these homes. [Pennings] had this thing worked out where he would provide housing for faculty and gave them money for coal and that sort of thing as part of their service for teaching at the college. Pennings ran the college in the early years. He bought some of these homes over the years. He didn't buy them all. But he owned a lot of property, which was pretty smart of him, around the periphery of the campus. What is now Burke Hall, on the river around the corner from Sensenbrenner, was built in [1942] and that's as far south as the campus went for a long period of time. Van Dyke was there forever.

The west side of Sensenbrenner would have been maybe 10 yards from Second Street. There also was a little street called Millar that came off Third and went to Second Street. Ed Longteau lived there. It would have been kitty-corner from Millar Street to Sensenbrenner. So when [the players] came out of that dormitory, Ed was there. Millar ran east and west, but it was only one block long. Ed's house actually was moved. It was moved on wheels down to Third Street. It's on the corner of High Street and Third now. [But back then], the players would have to cross Second Street to walk from Sensenbrenner to the Union for chow.

There were cars there, but not a lot. It was kind of like a cruiser street for anybody who was a BMC, big man on campus. You drove down Second Street to see what was happening. A lot of women would come over there when training camp was on. Occasionally, you'd see some kids. They'd want to get an autograph. But not like now. I didn't pay a whole lot of attention, but I'd see younger women driving up and down [Second Street] occasionally.

I can't certify it, but I was told Lombardi had a room in Main Hall in the southern tower. When you look at that building, there are two turrets. When I came for my visit, they had a guest room there and that's the room Lombardi used. I think Fr. Burke set that up for him. Burke's office was on the first floor; Lombardi's was up on the second floor, where the dean's office is now. At least, I was told that. A couple people told me, "Oh yeah, that's where Lombardi would stay." He had a great view from there. It could be part of myth and legend, but I was told that.

My brother-in-law was from Ohio and he played for the University of Dayton in basketball. He was a starter when they won the NIT, back in 1962. He'd come up and we'd go to training camp and watch a preseason game. One night we were sitting at Buck's tavern. There were many Packers who would go up there and have a libation. Elijah Pitts was there and I got to know him fairly well. My brother-in-law was amazed because at five minutes to 11, [Pitts] said, "I've got to get back," and he literally ran back to the dorm.

Buck's was a great place. I knew Buck Janssen very well. He was a great guy. He was a perfect gentleman, very unassuming, very quiet. I think he wanted civility in the place. It was a beautiful tavern. It had wainscoting. It was black with white sponging on it. It was almost a folk art kind of thing. Then they had the stamped metal tin all around the walls going up to the ceiling. Then the ceilings, of course, were stamped, too. And it was painted in three colors: white with gold embellishments, some touches of red and black around the bar. It was a great place to have a beer. I didn't see a lot of Packers in Buck's. But a lot of them knew it was a close place. I used to have a small seminar for students up there on Friday afternoon. It was a different world and there were many of us who did that. These Packers liked it because they knew it was the real deal.

I lived on Suburban Drive [in 1965]. I rented a house there. The funny thing was then if you saw an African-American going through West De Pere, everybody assumed he was a Packer. That's the way it was at that time. The college had some people of color on the faculty at that point who had some of their own difficulties, trying to rent a house and other things. They eventually got through that. But it was literally assumed that if you were black, you were a Packer.

The Science Hall [in 1965] was a World War II, barracks-like building. There's a sandlot volleyball court there right now. The building ran east and west. There were asphalt shingles on the outside walls, as well as the roof. It wasn't a classic Quonset hut, but it was built during World War II for training, I believe. The college was called Fort Norbert at that time by many people in the military. [The building] was really archaic and they finally tore it down. Maintenance used it for a long, long time after the Minahan Hall of Science was built. As I recall, the shingles on the outside were kind of a dirty red. It was really in sad shape.

DON GEORGE

George, a native of De Pere, owned Century Bowling Lanes & Bar from 1966 to 1972. Century Lanes was the Packers' favorite training camp hangout during the Lombardi era.

A certain bunch would come every day. I'd put cheese and crackers out. We served the beer in mugs with ice. They'd sit around the bar, drinking, listening to music. There was a pool table. They played pool, too. Sometimes they'd bowl.

They did it every year during training camp. When we bought the place that's where they had come. It was habit, I guess. Bart Starr would come. Zeke Bratkowski. Jerry Kramer. Bob Long. Bob Skoronski. Forrest Gregg. Gale Gillingham. Ken Bowman. Paul Hornung once in awhile. There'd be 15, 20 of them. They'd have to be back at St. Norbert before 6 o'clock.

I don't know if they went to other places or not. All I can tell you is that most of them came to the Century. I opened up for them. I wouldn't have been open at that time. I knew what time they'd get done with [practice] and I'd be ready. It would be about 5 o'clock.

We didn't encourage anyone else to come in, but some relation would come once in awhile and have a drink. But there wasn't too much interference.

Bart Starr would pick the tab up. He'd be there every day. He was the one who would write the songs down and tell me to get them on the juke box.

I started [the wall of autographs]. I asked them if they wanted to write their name on the wall. A new one would come in and I'd have him write on the wall. It was to the left [of the front door]. Right in the bar. I had a Packer flag up from when they won a championship. It was just a plain, plastered wall. How big an area? Maybe 8 feet by 12. I think it's still there.

JIM MAES

Maes' father, Vernon "Von" Maes, owned the bus company that provided the yellow school buses that transported the Packers from St. Norbert to the team's locker rooms at the stadium, and back, throughout the Lombardi era. Jim, on occasion, drove one of the buses. Maes Bus Service was in business from the early 1950s until the mid-1980s when it was sold to Lamers. Jim graduated from St. Norbert in 1959 and has lived on Fourth Street, near the campus, for more than 50 years.

We had school buses only, no coaches. I drove several times. We took them to the practice facility. I brought them out there; I brought them back. For the Bishop's Charities Game, we'd pick them up for the game and then after the game bring them back, too. I remember these big guys would come in, almost bumping their heads on the ceiling of the bus, and they'd just barely be moving. One step, then another step. They'd get partway down the bus and they'd sit on one side and put their feet across to the other side. School buses are pretty small seats. Then the next guy would come in and they'd argue about getting past them. They wouldn't step over their legs. They'd finally get in and then you'd see them on the field and they were running like crazy. You'd go, "Wait a minute. You were the same guys getting on the bus in the morning who could hardly move."

We just went out of De Pere on Ashland Avenue, then Ashland to what is now Lombardi, but was Highland Avenue then.

(Ashland was Highway 41 at the time. The 41 bypass that runs west of Ashland wasn't built until the mid-1970s.)

For a period of time, my dad leased the buses and [the players] drove them themselves. That didn't last long. They rough-housed them pretty bad. The buses were losing clutches and transmissions. They were driving them too fast and recklessly. And if there were breakdowns, they didn't know what to do.

My dad was in church a lot of mornings when [Lombardi] went to church at the Old St. Joe's church on the college campus.

GERRY OESTERREICH

Oesterreich sold newspapers to the Packers as a grade-school kid grow-ing up in West De Pere. He later delivered pizzas to them at Sensenbrenner Hall. A 1964 graduate of Pennings, he is a retired accountant, living in Lake Mills.

When I was going into seventh and eighth grade, I'd go down to the corner drug store, Stowe's, and buy newspapers. I'd get a half-dozen or so. I don't remember exactly, but I remember taking them to St. Norbert and selling them. I think the Press-Gazette was a dime then and I'd get a quarter [from the players]. Hornung was always good for a buck. I did that on my own. There were a couple of us who did it. That would be '59 and '60. I think we probably did it just about every day during training camp. In the summers going into seventh grade and eighth grade, I lived at 614 Third Street. The house isn't there anymore.

I was working for Bilotti's when I was delivering pizzas in the summer of '65. I delivered them into the dorms, probably 20 times in just one training camp. Never had any run-ins with any of the coaching staff. It was probably 9, 10, 11 o'clock. I don't recall what the tips were.

JIM GEVERS

Gevers cut hair at the family barber shop, located at 315 Main Ave. in West De Pere, for 43 years. Gevers started cutting hair in 1943, went into the service, returned to the shop in 1955 and retired in 1996.

The first year was when Scooter McLean [coached]. They were a bunch of misfits, a bunch of renegades. Ollie Spencer and J.D. Kimmel and some of those guys were so overweight. It was just a loose bunch. They'd come downtown with cutoff shorts up to the crack in their ass, bare-shirted, all that kind of stuff. The next year, Lombardi came and there was a transition like you couldn't believe. Everything was, "Yes, sir" and "No, sir," and long pants and shirts. Lenny Ford used to drink a case of Miller's beer after every practice.

He hung out I think at The Club tavern.

(Both Spencer and Kimmel, veteran tackles, played with the Packers in 1958, but were no longer with the team when camp opened in 1959. Ford had played eight years with the Cleveland Browns before the Packers obtained him. He was inducted into the Pro Football Hall of Fame in 1976, but he didn't even last the 1958 season with the Packers. McLean booted him off the team the night before the final game in Los Angeles.]

I think all [the Packers] came in [to the barber shop] at one time or another. I think the only two players who didn't come in during that whole era were Starr and Hornung. Emlen Tunnell would stop every single day and he had a feel for the pulse of the community. He got to know a lot of people, local people. Willie Davis was another one.

(Tunnell was a 37-year-old, 11-year veteran when Lombardi purchased him from the New York Giants in 1959. Although Tunnell was past his prime, he played three years in Green Bay and was a team leader. He was inducted into the Pro Football Hall of Fame in 1967.)

They'd come in for haircuts. There was a little restaurant next door and they didn't have cars. That was one reason they were around town. Guys like Tunnell and Jimmy Taylor and a couple guys would walk down and get a malted milk or something at the restaurant next door and then they'd stop in the shop and shoot the breeze or whatever. Then the bus would pick them up on the way out [to practice]. The restaurant was the Nicolet. It was called The Dairy Bar back then. It was a restaurant, but Ralph Meverden ran it and he made his own ice cream in the back. That's why they called it, The Dairy Bar. But by and large, they served breakfast and lunch. It was a full-scale restaurant. Dehn's was across the street and that's where the young people hung out; the Nicolet was the older crowd, the more mature crowd.

The time they'd stop in was early in the morning. They'd walk down after they had breakfast and before the bus left. A number of them would walk downtown and pick up a paper or stop in the shop and shoot the breeze. We had a number of guys who would stop in every morning.

[Main Avenue] was a two-way street and the bus driver would stop and two or three guys would get on the bus to go to practice. The same thing on the way home. When they'd get off the bus on the way home, those who weren't beer drinkers would stop and get a malt. Or they'd stop and get a haircut or have a few minutes to kill. Then they'd walk back to the college. It wasn't everybody, but there'd be a half-dozen or so.

There was the Ace Hi where they hung out. That was a favorite of theirs. It's Nicky's now. Beecher's was another place where guys hung out. It was down on Sixth Street, right next to where the Black & Tan was. Dave Hanner was a good friend of Art Beecher. A lot of guys went to Century Lanes. That was an evening or after practice place. There was Pete Janssen's tavern. Buck's came later. Those early, early years were when they were around town a lot because they didn't have a lot of cars around. The Tiny Tap was on the north side of the street.

[Tunnell was] a super guy. Very interesting. Very well read. Humor. The funny thing was he could tell by the practices what kind of game they'd have. The players really respected him. And so did the people. We hadn't had much exposure to blacks, but Emlen used to say, "This Green Bay is really something. Either you're, 'Hey, Willie!' Or 'Hey, Emlen!' They only know two names." I think Lombardi brought him in for a reason: his ability to understand and work with people. Like Lombardi, he was kind of a master psychologist. He had a feel for what was going on around here.

Lombardi would stop in. Interesting guy. If he wanted to talk a little bit, he'd leave his magazine or paper in the waiting chair. He liked to talk about his kids, liked to talk about golf; anything but football. And if he didn't want to talk, he'd bring the paper with him. Once camp was over, I think he had a friend, Joe Gryboski, who cut his hair. But during training camp, I cut his hair a number of times.

(Gryboski's barber shop was in the Northern Building, located at 301 E. Walnut St., in downtown Green Bay.)

The first year Lombardi was here, Timmy Brown was a kid from Ball State who went on to play with Philadelphia. We got a call one day and [the caller] said, "This is Mr. Lombardi." We thought somebody was putting us on. He said, "Do you have a color line down there at your barber shop?" We said, "No, no." I had been in the service and had cut black guys' hair before and felt a little comfortable, not that I was an expert at it. He said, "All right, I'm sending Timmy Brown down at 12 o'clock." We thought it was a joke and we weren't really prepared. All of a sudden, in walks this black kid, Timmy Brown. Of course, we had to take him even though there were a couple guys sitting around. It was well received, but they were kidding us after. "Cripes, players come to town and right away you take those guys ahead of us."

Back then they all had short hair. The blacks didn't have the shaved heads, but they had the close cropped hair. Jimmy Taylor got a haircut every 10 days, every two weeks for sure. Jimmy Taylor had a flattop, [Boyd] Dowler had a flattop. That was my forte back then. I had been in service and sometimes that was all I had done all day: cut flattops.

✤

Timeline of Lombardi's Training Camps

1959

July 23 – Rookies and more than a dozen veterans reported to the St. Norbert campus for a meeting and physicals. Two-a-day workouts were to start the next day and the entire team was scheduled to report July 25.

July 28 – Veteran fullback Howie Ferguson was traded to the Pittsburgh Steelers for an undisclosed draft choice. A week later, Ferguson was returned to the Packers due to a chronic shoulder injury. He would return to drills that summer, but then announce his retirement shortly before the season started.

Aug. 8 – The Blues beat the Whites, 28-7, in the Packers' intra-squad game, played before a paid crowd of 11,566 at what was then called new City Stadium. The highlight of the scrimmage was a 56-yard punt return by rookie Billy Butler, a native of Berlin, Wis., for the losing team.

Aug. 10 – The Packers ended two-a-day drills and began practicing just once at 10 a.m. But two meetings were scheduled each day at St. Norbert: one from 3 to 5 p.m., and the other from 7:15 to 9 p.m.

Aug. 15 – The Packers lost their exhibition debut under Vince Lombardi, falling to the Chicago Bears, 19-16, at Milwaukee County

Stadium. The Bears scored the winning touchdown with 41 seconds remaining on a 37-yard touchdown pass from quarterback Zeke Bratkowski to fullback Rick Casares.

Aug. 24 – Word leaked that safety Bobby Dillon, who had retired during the off-season, had informed the Packers that he had been given a leave of absence from his position as a sales manager for a plastics company in Texas and would return for one more season. For the past four years, Dillon had been chosen first-team all-NFL by the Associated Press. He reported to the Packers Sept. 1.

Aug. 26 – Veteran halfback Al Carmichael, who owned the NFL record for longest kickoff return, was waived.

Sept. 3 – Starting defensive tackle Jerry Helluin, an eight-year veteran, was waived.

Sept. 4 – The Packers broke camp at St. Norbert and headed east for exhibition games in Bangor, Maine, and Winston-Salem, N.C. When they returned, they spent five days at Oakton Manor on Pewaukee Lake, flew to Minneapolis for their final exhibition game, and then returned to Pewaukee for their final week of preparation before the season opener against the Bears. While in Bangor, Lombardi announced that tight end Ron Kramer, a first-round draft pick in 1957, had been discharged from the service and would join the team the following week.

Sept. 6 – After being discharged from the Army Reserves, second-year linebacker Ray Nitschke joined the Packers in Greensboro, N.C., where they were preparing for an exhibition game against the Washington Redskins.

Sept. 15 – The Packers announced in Pewaukee that they had acquired defensive tackle Henry Jordan from the Cleveland Browns in exchange for a draft choice. The draft pick turned out to be a fourth-rounder; Jordan went on to a Hall of Fame career. It also was announced that veteran quarterback Vito "Babe" Parilli had been waived.

1960

July 21 – Training camp officially opened as rookies and quarterbacks reported for lunch and physicals at St. Norbert. Two-a-day practices were scheduled to begin the next day. Veterans were scheduled to report July 23 and begin practice two days later.

Sept. 1 – A gust of wind knocked down the steel photographers' tower at the Packers' practice field and a large bolt punctured Nitschke's helmet, and pieces of scaffolding sent him sprawling. He escaped injury, but the accident could have been much more tragic. Only moments before, Nitschke had put on his helmet in anticipation of a thunderstorm.

Sept. 15 – The Packers moved out of St. Norbert and headed to Winston-Salem for their final exhibition game against the Redskins.

Sept. 17 – The Packers finished the preseason with a 6-0 record after crushing the Redskins, 41-7, as Bart Starr threw three touchdown passes.

1961

July 16 – Rookies, along with a handful of veterans, reported to St. Norbert for an evening meal and physicals. Two-a-day workouts were to start the next morning. Veterans were scheduled to report July 18.

July 18 – The immortal Don Hutson, still considered by some as the greatest Packer of all time, observed practice for the first time since he had resigned as an assistant coach following the 1948 season. Hutson played end for the Packers from 1935 to 1945 and was inducted into the Pro Football Hall of Fame as part of its charter class in 1963.

Aug. 5 – The Packers returned for the first time to old City Stadium, their home from 1925 to 1956, to play their annual intra-squad game and attracted a crowd of about 5,000. New City Stadium wasn't available because the turf had been reseeded.

Aug. 7 – Lombardi signed a new five-year contract at a noon news conference at St. Norbert College. It replaced the original five-year contract he signed in 1959. "Yeah, I'm a Badger now," Lombardi said with a laugh.

Aug. 8 – The Packers acquired quarterback John Roach from the Browns for an undisclosed draft pick. The Packers needed a veteran backup for Starr after Joe Francis injured his knee in the intra-squad game.

Sept. 4 – The Packers scored a 20-17 victory over the New York Giants before a record crowd of 33,452 in the first Bishop's Charities game. Paul Hornung kicked the winning field goal with 4:08 remaining. Bishop Stanislaus V. Bona threw out the first ball. The 2010 Bishop's Charities Game was the 50th annual.

Sept. 9 – The Packers beat the Redskins, 31-24, in Columbus, Ga., to finish the preseason 5-0.

1962

July 15 – Rookies and selected veterans reported to St. Norbert for physical exams and a meeting before starting two-a-day practices the next day. The schedule called for veterans to report July 17 and to start practice the next morning, but 19 of them reported with the rookies.

July 17 – The Packers traded veteran middle linebacker Tom Bettis to the Pittsburgh Steelers for an undisclosed draft choice.

July 24 – Halfback Paul Hornung, who won the NFL's Most Valuable Player Award the previous season, reported to camp after being discharged from the Army at Fort Riley, Kan.

Aug. 3 – Starr threw a record five touchdown passes as the Packers won the 29th annual College All-Star Game, 42-20, before 65,000 fans at

Soldier Field. The Packers gave the game ball to Ernie Davis, the 1961 Heisman Trophy winner who had been recently hospitalized and unable to play for the All-Stars. Davis was subsequently diagnosed with leukemia and died within a year.

Aug. 12 – While in Dallas following an exhibition game, the Packers traded rookie halfback Ernie Green, a 14th-round draft choice out of Louisville, to the Browns for an undisclosed draft pick. Green was impressive in camp, but was fourth-string on the talent-rich Packers. The Browns needed a replacement for Davis and Green filled the bill, rushing for more than 3,000 yards in his career.

Sept. 8 – The Packers edged the Redskins, 20-14, at Columbus, Ga., to finish the preseason 6-0.

1963

July 14 – Rookies, plus 12 veterans, reported to St. Norbert for the start of camp. Two-a-day practices were to start the next day. Remaining veterans were to report the night of July 16 and start practice the next day.

Aug. 1 – It was reported that the Packers and Redskins had agreed to move their exhibition game, scheduled for Sept. 7 in Columbus, Ga., to Cedar Rapids, Iowa, because fans in the stands would have had to have been segregated by race and there was some fear of demonstrations. Earlier in Lombardi's tenure, when the Packers played exhibition games in the South, there were times when the team's black players had to stay some place other than the team hotel. But prior to the 1962 exhibition game in Columbus, Lombardi had the Packers stay at nearby Fort Benning so whites and blacks could stay together.

Aug. 2 – Quarterback Ron VanderKelen and end Pat Richter, former University of Wisconsin teammates, connected on a 74-yard touchdown pass in the fourth quarter for what proved to be the winning touchdown as the College All-Stars shocked the Packers, 20-17, before 65,000 fans at Soldier Field. VanderKelen, a Green Bay native, completed 9 of 11 passes for 141 yards and was named MVP of the All-Stars.

Aug. 8 – Gary Knafelc, who spent nine years with the Packers and started at tight end during Lombardi's first two seasons, announced his retirement and was waived. Three weeks later, Knafelc signed with the San Francisco 49ers.

Sept. 10 – The Packers broke camp at St. Norbert.

1964

July 15 – Rookies, quarterbacks and some other eager veterans reported to camp and were to begin two-a-days the next day. The remaining veterans were to report July 19 and start practice the next day.

Aug. 1 – Hornung, returning from a year's suspension for gambling, was the star of the annual intra-squad game played before an estimated 27,000 fans at new City Stadium. The offense beat the defense, 16-9, as Hornung rushed for 61 yards in eight carries and caught three passes for 64 yards.

Sept. 7 – The Packers broke camp at St. Norbert.

1965

July 21 – Rookies and all veteran skill position players reported for physicals at St. Norbert and started practicing the next day. Veteran linemen were required to report July 24 with the first full practice for the entire team scheduled for July 26. On the afternoon of the 21st, hours before camp opened, Lombardi played golf with Jack Nicklaus in a charity event at Oneida Golf and Riding Club. Nicklaus shot a par 72; Lombardi, 82. Former Packers' great Don Hutson and Oneida pro Bill Furnari were the others in the foursome.

July 26 – Veteran tackle Norm Masters retired after eight seasons with the Packers. Masters had basically shared the left tackle position with Bob Skoronski since 1959, but also had played full time when injuries hit.

Aug. 3 – The Packers were awarded a first-round draft pick as compensation after it was announced that Ron Kramer, who had played out his option the previous year, had signed with Detroit.

Aug. 14 – NFL Commissioner Pete Rozelle spoke to the Packers' players in the afternoon and attended the annual Bishop's Charities Game at night. The Packers trounced the New York Giants, 44-7.

Sept. 11 – In a brief pre-game ceremony prior to the Packers' final exhibition game of the summer, what was formerly known as City Stadium was renamed Lambeau Field in honor of the team's longtime coach, Curly Lambeau, who had died of a heart attack three months earlier. In the game that followed, the Packers beat the St. Louis Cardinals, 31-13. That same day, defensive tackle Dave Hanner retired after 13 seasons with the Packers. Hanner remained with the team as an assistant coach.

1966

July 13 – Rookies and veteran skill-position players reported to camp for dinner and physicals. Two-a-day drills were to start the next day and the veteran offensive and defensive linemen were to report July 16.

Aug. 5 – The Packers tied the record for the most lopsided victory in the 33-year history of the College All-Star Game, crushing the All-Stars, 38-0, before 72,000 fans at Soldier Field. Playing against the Packers were their two prized rookie backs, Donny Anderson and Jim Grabowski, but neither did much. Anderson left with an ankle injury in the second quarter; Grabowski carried four times for 13 yards.

Sept. 6 – The Packers moved out of St. Norbert to mark the end of camp.

1967

July 12 – Rookies and all veterans other than linemen reported and took their physicals at Lambeau Field. The linemen were scheduled to join the rest of the team at St. Norbert July 15.

July 23 – Grabowski, who was expected to replace Taylor at fullback, reported to camp after completing a six-month stint in the Army at Fort Leonard Wood, Mo.

July 26 – Anderson, the heir apparent to Hornung, reported to camp following six months in the National Guard at Camp Ripley, Minn.

Aug. 4 – For the second straight year, the Packers buried the College All-Stars, 27-0, before a crowd of 70,934 at Soldier Field. Grabowski, fresh off 48 hours of National Guard duty as the result of racial riots in Milwaukee, rushed for 77 yards in nine carries and scored a touchdown on a 22-yard run.

Sept. 10 – The Packers broke camp at St. Norbert following a Sunday morning breakfast. The night before, they beat the New York Giants, 31-14, at Lambeau to finish 6-0, their first unbeaten preseason since 1962.

1968

(Lombardi had resigned as coach following the 1967 season.)
July 10 – Lombardi, general manager of the Packers and also a member of NFL management's negotiating team, announced that the Packers' training camp at St. Norbert would be open only to rookies as the result of the stalemate in labor negotiations between owners and players. Lombardi acted in accordance with other NFL owners, who had decided to lock out the veterans.

July 15 – The Packers veterans started reporting to camp and practiced for the first time after NFL owners and players had settled their pension dispute the night before.

Aug. 1 – Lombardi said a new Packers' policy assigning rooms to rookies based on alphabetical order, regardless of race, was decided upon a year ago. Two black rookies, Leon Crenshaw and John Robinson, were rooming with whites, Brendan McCarthy and Dick Himes, as a result of the new policy. Veterans Jerry Kramer and Willie Davis also requested to room together. The plan was to also assign another black, first-round draft pick Fred Carr, a white roommate when he reported from the College All-Star Game.